MASTERING

Focus Groups and

Depth Interviews

MASTERING
Focus Groups and Depth Interviews

A Practitioner's Guide

Roger A. Straus, Ph.D.

Paramount Market Publishing, Inc.

Paramount Market Publishing, Inc.
274 North Goodman Street, STE D-214
Rochester, NY 14607
www.paramountbooks.com
Phone: 607-275-8100

Publisher: James Madden
Editorial Director: Doris Walsh

ISBN 13: 978-1-941688-66-3 | ISBN 10: 1-941688-65-9
eISBN 13: 978-1-941688-67-0

DEDICATION AND ACKNOWLEDGMENT

I'd like to dedicate this volume both to my amazingly supportive and talented wife, Kathryn Frederick, and to Alfred E. Goldman, my first marketing research guru.

I would also like to acknowledge the critical role of Carey Azzara, who encouraged me to write a practical guide to doing focus groups and published the initial version of this volume as an eBook.

Contents

Introduction

Focus groups and depth interviews. They weren't on the curriculum, even in the qualitatively oriented graduate program in sociology I fell into at the University of California, Davis. Using social science methods in the real world, or even worse in business settings? Nah — cut to the scene in Monty Python's *Life of Brian* with all those toga-clad officials going around crying, "Unclean! Unclean!"

Who knew that qualitative methods pioneered by sociologists were actually being used in marketing research and other applied settings? Virtually anybody who did wasn't talking about it. And, in any case, while some survey researchers were clinging to their identity as sociologists, it seemed that the great majority of marketing researchers and those in other applied social science fields, like organizational development, had psychology backgrounds. So they wouldn't know.

Even years later, when I left university teaching to become a marketing researcher, all I knew about this profession was the name, and that only because a colleague had left the Psychology Department and told us he had been recruited by a business school to teach "market research," whatever that meant. I was familiar with intensive interviews and trained in qualitative analysis. In fact, my first professional publication, originally written as part of my doctoral program, was based on a series of intensive interviews.

But, although I had received post-graduate training (and a doctoral specialization) in qualitative sociology from some of its leading lights, I'd never heard of "focus groups" or "depth interviews" as practiced by applied researchers. I had no inkling that these methodologies were essentially originated just before World War II by Columbia University sociologists affiliated with its Bureau of Applied Social Research, along with modern survey research, or that they were coming to be widely used in applied and business contexts.

When I was ready to leave my academic position at Alfred University in far-Western New York State, I saw a notice in the American Sociological Association's *Employment Bulletin* seeking experienced researchers interested in doing marketing research. I had already started an applied track in my sociology department, co-founded what is now the Association for Applied and Clinical Sociology, gone around the country promoting the idea of sociological practice at professional conferences (to the consternation of many very senior academics), even served as President of the American Sociological Association's Section on Sociological Practice.

So, figuring, "What the heck?" I flew down to Philadelphia and was hired that very day by Al Goldman, who, it turns out, had pioneered the use of focus groups with physicians and other professionals at National Analysts, at the time a division of the consulting firm, BoozAllen Hamilton.

After observing and analyzing a bunch of depth interviews, I was sent off to do some on my own. As I recall, my first day of interviewing was at a Chicago facility directly above a beauty salon, with vapors of hair dye and permanent-product waves wafting up into the interview room. It was fairly easy, if somewhat intimidating, to transfer the qualitative research skills I had learned in graduate school to interviewing physicians about pharmaceuticals and other medical topics.

But focus groups were, along with quantitative segmentation, one of our firm's premiere specialties. Our cash cows. Not just anybody was allowed to do focus groups. You had to earn the right to do them.

I have never received any formal training or certification in doing focus groups. Rather, for maybe a year, Al had me observe his groups and take notes in the back room, then analyze the results and write up reports before I was allowed to do my first group on my own — and what a group it was. AZT (the first AIDS drug) had just received its indication for treatment of asymptomatic HIV disease. At the time, Burroughs Wellcome — the manufacturer — was hated by the HIV community for its homophobic Good Old Boy leadership and how they were handling this horrible epidemic. So I found myself in a basement conference room at the Washington D.C. Hyatt Regency with a tape recorder on the table, a bunch of HIV-positive lawyers, a totally freaked-out young sailor with AIDS, and our head client, a Director from Burroughs in the same room. That was a trial by fire!

Over a quarter century and many hundreds of groups and interviews later, I was asked by Carey Azzara to write an eBook for his online marketing education and training program. Our goal was to provide a truly practical guide for focus group moderators and those who work with moderators — step by step, from the ground up. I was only marginally aware of the many other settings in which focus groups were being employed.

Granted, I had led conference sessions introducing my fellow sociological practitioners to focus groups and focus group methodology, I'd personally done groups as part of employee research programs, and I knew that a variation was widely employed by legal researchers for mock juries. Still, I'd been insulated from focus groups' uses in other non-business settings. In this updated and expanded version, I hope to correct that and expand the book to be useful to practitioners and users of focus groups outside of just the marketing research context — basically anyone who uses or wants to use focus groups for applied research — although I will still largely focus my stories and examples on marketing research as it's what I know best.

Originally, the plan was to put out a second eBook on depth interviewing, but that never came to pass. In the course of preparing this volume, I realized that such a book would be largely redundant; most of what I have to say about focus groups applies to understanding, doing, and analyzing applied depth interviews. So I decided to make this a "once and done" guide to the theory and practice of both. This volume is, in effect, my Masterwork, in the original sense of the term.

As the first chapter will detail, focus groups and depth interviews are not the be-all and end-all of qualitative marketing and social research, but represent two basic tools of applied qualitative research along with ethnography, participant observation, and other, technology-enabled methods such as "online bulletin boards." The remainder of Part 1 goes into more detail on the nature and uses of focus groups and depth interviews, mainly from the perspective of the research practitioner, but it is also intended to provide an in-depth introduction for anyone who uses, attends, or commissions focus group research.

Part 2 covers focus group and depth interview planning and preparation for high impact. Part 3 shows you how to translate all of these principles and plans into action, how to moderate focus groups and depth interviews, concluding with two chapters on how to analyze depth research.

My approach is deliberately pragmatic, discussing how to design focus groups and depth interviews, including overall research design, discussion guides, and dealing with clients. Again, while these sections are written with the practitioner in mind, sharing what I have experienced and learned in my decades as a marketing research and sociological practitioner, they are designed to have the latent function of empowering readers who commission, use, and collaborate with applied qualitative researchers.

I trust that you will find this book interesting, valuable, and even enjoyable. Feel free to contact me at any time with questions or comments through the publisher or at:

rogerstraus@gmail.com
August 2019
West Linn, Oregon

PART 1

NATURE AND USES OF DEPTH RESEARCH

CHAPTER 1

Depth Interviews and Focus Groups:

What They Are and What They Aren't

Depth interviews and focus groups (which I will refer to collectively as "depth research") are, without doubt, the best-known and most widely deployed methods of applied qualitative research. They are used in a variety of settings such as marketing research, social science research, program evaluation, employee research, mock trials/legal research, community development, and public opinion and political research.

A **depth interview** is an intensive, semi-structured guided conversation between a moderator and a single individual during a pre-arranged time-frame to explore one or more topics, ideas, products, programs, services, situations — virtually anything for which you seek qualitative intelligence. A depth interview is interactive, guided, and somewhat free-flowing in contrast to **structured interviews** that adhere to a strict script and employ close-ended, multiple-choice or fill-in-the-blank short answer questions. A depth interview is similar to psychological or psychiatric interviews with respect to seeking deep insight through open-ended questions (that's where "depth" comes from), but its purpose is to meet specific informational versus therapeutic objectives. Not, however, "just the facts" as in journalism. The goal is to go deeper than that, to achieve what we sociologists term *verstehen*, which the Oxford dictionary defines as "empathic understanding of human behavior."*

---

* *https://en.oxforddictionaries.com/definition/verstehen*

A **focus group** is also a moderator-facilitated informational discussion but conducted with a group of individuals. The key difference from depth interviews is you bring together and interview four or more individuals as a group, versus bringing them together in the same place at the same time and interviewing them as individuals. In other words, as my mentor Al Goldman put it, a focus group is a *group depth interview* (1962). The group setting adds a number of demands and dynamics that make it more difficult to master than individual depth interviews, but the basic principles are the same.

Focused, Informational

Depth methods are different from other types of interviews and "discussion groups" in that they are focused — explicitly designed and managed to obtain targeted information or intelligence (Merton, Kendall and Gollin, 1990). If they do not accomplish that objective, they are a failure.

Let's be clear from the outset: whatever you might see in TV ads, a depth interview or focus group is not a promotional event, conducted to spread the word about a product, brand, company, political candidate, program, policy, or anything else. It is not a vehicle to propagandize or persuade people to a specific point of view, nor a staged event to create consideration and promote sales. Clients or sponsors may have those objectives, while advertisers have taken to portraying pseudo-focus-groups as a "voice of the customer" gimmick, but practitioners consider "marketing under the guise of research" to be a veritable sin.

Similarly, depth interviews and focus groups are not the proper format to provide therapeutic experience or group therapy. While participants may gain insight into their problems or issues, and may experience relief from stresses, anxieties, sense of isolation, and stigmatization from sharing with others in the same position as themselves, these are occasional side benefits. While a very positive outcome for all involved, this is at best secondary to the informational or exploratory purpose of the research.

Moderated

A depth interview or focus group is intensively moderated. It is not a free discussion of a topic or issue. It's not what you'd see in a speakers' panel, political forum, or professional conference session where a "moderator" facilitates some kind of discussion or presentation, nor the type of interview a journalist would conduct. Depth research is, indeed, a kind of discussion and can be described as being "facilitated" by the moderator — but in a very specific, deliberately structured and directive way. It's not a matter of getting a person to answer a series of questions or having one person speak first and then another, even if about a particular topic.

The moderator runs and manages the session following a specific, detailed plan. This can be done in-person, online, or possibly by phone. The moderator not only asks questions but (to borrow the language of theater) serves as prompter, director, stage manager, even while himself or herself taking and performing the role of questioner and gentle interrogator for the interviewee(s) and, ultimately, the audience of clients and others who may be observing in real time, or through recordings or transcripts. Compare this with a structured interview in which an interviewer asks a series of short-answer questions in a predefined order, perhaps with one or two probes for completeness.

There's a lot of craft, technique, and, yes, showmanship involved. Moderating is one of many things that sets depth research apart from a simple process of Q&A or facilitating a panel discussion.

Although in the depth interview setting the person asking questions is usually referred to as an "interviewer," what they actually do is to moderate more than just facilitate. A focus group moderator's role is more complex in that he or she presides over and facilitates the group, posing questions and prompting participants to respond not only to their questions but also to other group members. In both cases, the moderator steers the discussion to keep it on track, to ensure that the individual interviewee or all group members participate fully and unreservedly, and to ensure that the sponsor's agenda is met (even if that is purely informational). As I have emphasized, unlike other types of interviews and what are sometimes, improperly, called "focus groups," depth research is actively directed toward predetermined research objectives — it's not a matter of "whatever."

Group depth interviews

A depth interview is conducted with one interviewee and involves facilitating an intensive one-on-one relationship. A true focus group is moderated among a group of individuals. The term, group depth interview, was originated by Al Goldman (1962), who pioneered use of commercial focus groups with physicians and other professionals. His point was that the group is being interviewed, not the individuals sitting around the table.

The moderator facilitates interaction in order to harness the power of group dynamics and dig deeper than individuals' initial surface responses. It is the moderator's first task to facilitate, rapidly, the consolidation of this set of strangers into a group. The whole thing is held together by and, indeed, runs on the interactions among group members and between them and the moderator.

A focus group is not just a set of serial interviews between the moderator and the individual participants. This distinction between a group depth interview and a serial interview is critical. One doesn't go around the table asking each person their opinion in turn. I once was fired from a focus group project on medication for ADHD by a client who was upset that I didn't go around the table and ask each of the 12 parents the same question in turn, as if I were doing a quantitative survey or serial interview. I probably should have briefed the clients in advance to set expectations. When working with new clients who are not very familiar with you or focus groups, I suggest you do that.

A seasoned moderator asks questions and directs activities, continually probing for "why" and "what else?" You do that also in depth interviews, but to obtain true depth of response the focus group moderator adds strategic guidance of the interactions among group members. Establishing, channeling and directing group dynamics, in other words. That's the key to getting respondents to forget about the fact that they are in a focus group, to take off their social "masks" and stop "playing to the audience" of the moderator, their peers, and whoever is behind the one-way mirror or watching remotely. A well-moderated group is arguably the best way to surface participants' true points of view, along with the whys behind what they say or do. Individual interviews may maximize depth and breadth of information but groups can maximize depth of understanding.

For example, in a group of parents, the moderator might throw out a question to the group, "Okay, you say that you are concerned about the fact that this ADHD medication is a form of methamphetamine, why do you say that?" and "Jane, what do you think of what Bill just told us about this?" Alternatively, "Bill, Jane's shaking her head; please explain what you are thinking to her." Or Sarah might spontaneously say to Harry, "Oh come on, my kid is able to study and not be disruptive, it's almost the opposite of what meth-heads are like when they use the stuff to get high." Harry might counter with, "I don't know, back in high school some of my classmates used to save up their ADHD meds and sell them to others who used them to get high."

This is why my general preference is for focus groups over depth interviews, all things being equal. Social psychologists (including me) would argue, like the English poet John Donne that "No man is an island." We are all members of social systems, the most basic of which are our groups, starting with our birth family. Our membership defines our identities and influences what we do and say; hence, a focus group provides a window into this dynamic.

While Goldman, a clinical psychologist by training, developed his approach to focus groups in the late 1950s, the technique is quite a bit older than that. It is based on the "focused interview" technique pioneered by the eminent sociologist, Robert K. Merton at Columbia University's Bureau of Applied Social Research in the early 1940s. "Focused interviews" were essentially the same as what we are calling depth interviews, but from early on, researchers began applying the same basic approach to working with groups of consumers or others and the *focus group* was born. Liza Featherstone

(2018) has recently documented the origins and subsequent history of focus groups in detail.

Synchronous

Both depth interviews and focus groups are conducted with a preselected, screened, and qualified set of research subjects interacting together at the same time, that is, synchronously. Until recently, this was pretty much a given, but digital technology has made it seem almost quaint to the newest cohorts of qualitative researchers.

Some now use the term "online focus groups" to describe a methodology in which people individually record their thoughts and comments in real time or later onto a virtual bulletin board or similar platform, each at a time of their choosing on a 24/7 basis over a matter of days or even months. Thus, unlike a true focus group, such methods are "*asynchronous*."

While this approach can be extremely valuable as a methodological option, it is not a true focus group, although it draws on many of the same design and moderating skills and could be combined with actual focus groups. In the past few years, I have done quite a few of these studies and have become quite a partisan, but they represent a different tool than focus groups, with their own dynamics, needs, benefits, and challenges. Dale and Abbott (2014) provide a good overview of online qualitative methods.

Qualitative research vs. quantitative research

Stepping back to another basic point, there is a lot of confusion among users and even researchers regarding the difference between qualitative and quantitative research. *Focus groups and depth interviews yield qualitative insight, not quantitative data* (although one can obtain at least rough quantitative insight if one does enough focus groups or interviews, as I'll discuss below).

Time and again, the applied qualitative researcher must deal with the consequences of that misunderstanding. For example, much of the literature on marketing research and other potential applications for focus groups and depth interviews — both scientific and popular or business-directed — disparages qualitative research as a basis for decision making compared to more "scientific" and "representative" quantitative research. After all, this argument claims, qualitative research is subjective, depth inquiry cannot be exactly replicated (unlike standardized quantitative survey questions), and different analysts can come to different conclusions from the same qualitative material; that is, it lacks "intersubjective certifiability." Qualitative samples are small and not randomly selected.

Essentially, these critics don't understand that qualitative and quantitative research fall into separate methodological domains.

It is, perhaps, easiest to define qualitative research by contrast with what it is not: quantitative research. Quantitative research obtains and analyzes data, that is, numbers, measurements, rates and ratios, and so forth. It counts and measures things, providing the basis for statistical analysis and modeling. Highly formalized, it fits what most people think of as "objective" or "scientific." Qualitative research, in contrast, is open-ended, exploratory, sensitizing. Rather than seeking to establish "objective" and definitive facts or answers, it focuses on discovery — uncovering people's realities, finding out what's going on, how and why people feel, think and behave as they do. Qualitative material should be analyzed qualitatively, and there are rigorous and systematic ways of doing it, as will be discussed later.

"Qualitative" is almost a pun, in that it gets at what it's like for people, their motives and motivations, the subjective and experiential as much or more than the objective "facts of the matter." It is used to discover patterns, themes and variations versus testing hypotheses and determining cause-and-effect or statistical relationships. That is, to gain *verstehen* into some aspect of human life and reality. To use the highly popular metaphor, it is more right-brained than left-brained.

While many do not, at least some clients and researchers "get" qualitative research and appreciate the proper role of qualitative methods. For example, I met with the newly appointed chief fundraiser for a major university's endowment. She complained that they have years of survey data describing trends, measuring the results of campaigns, identifying what did and didn't work. However, they have absolutely no sense of the whys behind any of this. She asked for a series of focus groups to explore, for example, why a recent solicitation fell flat on its face. What went wrong? Why did only about one percent of the prospective donors targeted respond, when historically at least ten times that number typically do? Did they throw the direct mail solicitation away, unread? Did they open and scan it and not recognize that it was from their alma mater? How did they do what they did and why? Why? Why? This is a classic example of a properly made call for depth research.

CHAPTER 2

Depth Methods: What Are They Good For?

Can we trust what we learn from qualitative research like focus groups or depth interviews? Is it as "good" — reliable, valid, trustworthy, and actionable — as the information we can obtain from quantitative surveys and the like? As implied in the last chapter, this is often framed as an either/or question comparing qualitative versus quantitative research. Rather than get into a technical discussion invoking the philosophy of science with lots of multi-syllabic jargon, let's look at it pragmatically.

Identifying patterns vs. statistical relationships

Qualitative research is best at discovering patterns, getting into customers' and prospects' "heads" to gain insight into reality as they perceive it, for understanding how and why people act as they do, and identifying what one might call the "deep structure" of the things humans do. This extends to understanding what people mean by their words and actions, their semantics and even pragmatics of communication (Mira 2010). Quantitative research is best for measuring things, testing specific hypotheses, evaluating relationships among observed phenomena, cause-effect relationships in particular.

The bottom line is that quantitative and qualitative research yield different kinds of information and insights. They are essentially complementary.

"I want some interviews/focus groups"

Whether one works in a research or marketing unit within a larger organization, within some other type of consultancy or setting, or as an external research supplier (in a market research, applied social science, public agency or other context), it is not uncommon that someone will contact you and say, "I want some interviews," or "I want some focus groups."

I have seen quite a few requests that simply read something like, "We have a new product of (whatever type) and we want to do some focus groups with potential customers." Well, you'd have to ask at least a few questions to figure out who to interview, about what, for what purpose, and probably prepare some kind of proposal. At other times, potential clients send out formal RFPs (requests for proposals) that go into great detail about process issues, perhaps list specific questions they want addressed, identify a strict timeline, and request pricing (all too often assuming that everything can be broken down into hourly rates multiplied by number of hours). Sometimes these are more informal, verbal requests, although that is increasingly rare in these days of bureaucracy, procurement units, and digital communication. One can simply give internal or external clients what they request. Then go ahead and do whatever the clients say they want.

There are, without a doubt, many researchers who will do just that. While this "order-taker" approach might be the easiest way to go, it is really a dereliction of duty on the researcher's part. You might score points and even jobs by doing whatever you are asked to do, but you're not very likely to help the clients get what they really need.

Increasingly budget-conscious 21st century businesses, agencies, and non-profits, are less tolerant than they once were of mediocre, off-target research. They are certainly not going to support research for research's sake. Research is expected to provide a meaningful return on investment, just like marketing and every other corporate function. In the past couple of years, the expectation has shifted in many cases from just seeking actionable information to producing "insights" (of which I'll speak more in a later chapter).

A professional recognizes that any research methodology is just a tool. The purpose of a tool is to help the user get something done. The purpose of marketing research is to give the decision maker the information needed to make the best possible business decision.

Other applications of depth interviews and focus groups, from applied social science through mock juries, employee research, and so forth have similarly practical objectives. However, just because you can offer depth methods at least as part of a research program, as many of us learned back in shop classes, it all goes back to the tried and true principle, "use the right tool for the job."

Focus groups or individual interviews?

That brings me to another question. How do you choose between focus groups and individual depth interviews? Where does each of these synchronous methods fit?

Focus Groups

Focus groups have markedly different dynamics than individual interviews. In my experience, they offer greater breadth of learnings and maximize your "bang for the buck." The "group" in "group depth interview" enables you to more effectively test concepts (the idea kind as well as marketing, product and program designs, advertising, or promotional "concepts"), get directly to exploring areas of consensus or disagreement, and get the big picture. By leveraging group dynamics you're better able to dig into the unknown, discover what you didn't know enough or think to inquire about, get a better sense of what goes on in people's real-world lives (or the equivalent for groups and organizations), simulate what you can expect to happen in the social world, and tap the power of interaction to maximize creativity.

Focus groups are particularly useful for exploration and discovery.

1. Focus groups are particularly useful when scoping out topics, issues, markets, and situations that are new to you and your clients or about which you do not know enough to ask all the questions necessary to meet your research objectives. They enable you to understand how your target audiences are likely to think and feel, their language, their attitudes, and behaviors.

2. If they are conducted as the first phase of a qualitative-quantitative research project, they can provide the foundation you need to develop truly effective surveys (field tests or other experiments). For example, what you can learn in a relatively few focus groups can enable you to write closed-ended or multiple-choice questions that cover all necessary bases, and do so in the language and mental frame of your subjects.

Peer-to-peer interaction "keeps it real."

3. In a focus group, group dynamics can be leveraged by an adept moderator to allow group members to challenge one another and their self-presentations, test their beliefs about "how things really are," uncover taken-for-granted realities of their lives, and surface the unknown and unexpected.

Human beings are not isolated individuals. We are all connected as members of the multiple social systems (groups, organizations, cultures, societies) within which we carry out our lives according to our roles and status within these systems. This might seem to be a sociological generalization, but it has direct impact on our actual behavior. When a focus group is comprised of peers (at least as participants see it), each group member can serve as a reality check on what others in the group say or claim to do. At the same time, their very presence can prompt members to stay "in character" and act in a way that is likely to represent how they will think, feel, or behave in real world settings according to their social roles, statuses, and culture.

In everyday social interaction, we put a lot of effort into maintaining our social "masks." That is, presenting ourselves as we desire to be perceived and responded to, in accordance with our social roles, status, desired self-image, and so on. (Goffman, 1959). Whoever and whatever we are, we are always "on stage" with respect to others. While this is especially significant when working with high-status individuals — doctors, lawyers, or executives, it is true of everyone.

Group depth interviewing

4. Group depth interviewing also minimizes time and hassle for the researcher and the client and can reduce overall time in the field compared with individual interviews.

5. On the other hand, you will obtain less information and less depth of information from each participant than you can get from one-on-one interviews. Think about it: if you have eight participants and conduct a two-hour (120 minute) group and moderate the session so that everyone contributes equally, you can get an average of about fifteen minutes' input per person (actually less, taking into account the time required to moderate, and for logistics).

Some questions or topics are unsuitable for focus group exploration.

6. Groups are also problematic when exploring or addressing sensitive or potentially embarrassing topics, when putting together people of very different statuses (socioeconomic, organizational, educational) or lifestyles, or competitors and others who would be unwilling or uncomfortable revealing "trade secrets" or the like to one another.

Focus groups can save time and money vs. depth interviews.

7. When doing research in the specialized central facilities generally employed for commercial research, you can generally get away with a lower budget if you do a few evenings of groups vs. days and days of depth interviews, but you can also more easily do individual interviews on a shoestring budget.

Individual depth interviews

Depth interviews obtain a greater quantity of information from each interviewee than one can get from focus group members. There are a lot of upsides.

They are, however, subject to a lot of constraints with respect to discovery and serendipity. You work from a discussion guide that is based on what you (your team, or your clients) know and are already aware of. Additionally, the social situation of the interview creates a structured demand situation. Basically you ask a question and the interviewee responds to that question. An interviewer quickly establishes the respective roles of the asker and the asked and creates rapport between them. Yes, you can probe for more and possibly discover the unexpected. However, the usual depth or intensive interview follows that pre-defined line of questioning.

Furthermore, the one-on-one setting tends to maintain a kind of separation between the interviewer and the interviewee that enables the interviewees to engage in "facework" (Goffman, 1959). They act to present themselves as they wish to be seen by the interviewer, to censor their responses, say what they might think or consider they should or would like the interviewer to perceive that they do, believe, or feel.

There are some specific needs or situations that can tilt the balance toward selecting individual interviews:

When you need or want more individual depth than you can obtain with groups.

8. You can get 30 minutes' to an hour's worth of information from any single participant in a one-on-one interview versus an average of perhaps 13 minutes per participant in an eight-person, two-hour group.
9. Focus groups may be a better choice when you need to explore and discover behavior or attitudinal patterns, what's going on, or how things work.

When budget is the driving issue.

10. Another factor is that, you can possibly save money if you can do one-on-one interviews in informal settings which are not generally suitable for groups.

When dealing with diverse and/or very rare informants.

11. Depth interviews are the better choice when there are many distinct, clearly defined segments or subgroups that either would not fit together in a single focus group or from which you seek deep understanding

at the segment/sub-segment level (vs. overall). Similarly, individual interviews are often more practical when you would be hard-pressed to find enough people of a desired type to assemble a group in any one location or enough of each type for remote (e.g., online) groups to be practical.

When your target audiences may not be compatible.

12. For example, when you need to interview direct competitors or antagonists who would not be comfortable or possibly even willing to participate in the same group, or else high-status individuals such as C-level executives, senior-level administrators, experts or thought leaders who would want the attention and respect implicit in a one-on-one interview vs. a group.

If the research topic or discussion may involve very sensitive, private, likely embarrassing topics, or disclosures.

13. The research might reveal trade or business secrets and other information participants would be unwilling or uncomfortable sharing with peers in a focus group.

    There are some techniques that are better suited to depth interviews than groups Advanced projective methods can require intensive interaction between the moderator and participant and/or intense concentration on the interviewee's part. Anything that requires intense rapport between interviewer and interviewee or requires participants to concentrate intensely is best suited to the individual depth interview vs. groups setting.

Some clients favor one-on-one interviews over groups.

14. This could be due, for example, to familiarity, poor experiences with focus groups and focus group moderators. Over time, it appears that the relative preference for groups vs. depth interviews and vice versa varies much like a fad.

To obtain better quality, more detailed video documentation from individual interviews than from groups.

15. When you or your client will want to present professional or near-

professional quality clips or videos. "Stationary" videos of focus groups may capture individuals to some extent but as part of the group, while many online group platforms can only yield thumbnail images of participants and their responses. Although you can bring in a videographer to obtain higher quality video in either groups or depth interviews, the latter allows for clear focus on the individual vs. occasional "cameos" of multiple group members.

In summary, each form of depth research has its place in the qualitative researcher's toolkit; basically, individual interviews for depth of information and detail about individual segments or sub-segments, focus groups when you want to obtain insight or understand patterns at a more general group or segment level, and to be able to directly observe similarities and differences within and among them, to maximize serendipity, save time and hassle (it takes longer to interview the same number of people individually vs. in groups), but are willing to obtain less individual depth of information.

Here's a practical guide to determining which approach is best for any specific research project, depth interviews or focus groups:

Individual Interviews or Groups?

	Individual Interviews	Focus Groups
Seek to Maximize	Amount/depth of information from each participant Understanding of between-segment differences Representation of distinct target segments	Overall insight/themes and variations Serendipity/discovery Time- and cost-efficiency
Going-in Knowledge/ Familiarity	Adequate to develop comprehensive guide	Little to uncertain Many unknowns
Target Informants	Numerous distinct types/segments with strict eligibility criteria Hard-to-find or recruit/low incidence Competitors/high status individuals	Can break into small number of relatively homogeneous segments/groupings Can find/recruit up to 16 per group session No direct competitors

	Individual Interviews	Focus Groups
Information Sensitivity	Very sensitive, private Potentially embarrassing Trade/personal secrets, other confidential information	Shareable within a group of peers Not too embarrassing to share with peers Disclosure/secrecy not an issue or concern
Required Concentration, Participant Engagement	Can be strong-to-intense	Moderate at most
Use of Recordings	Detailed high-grade individual videos to show/analyze	Group videos/thumbnails to show/analyze

Problem vs. technique-based approach

As any marketing or business research textbook will emphasize, the purpose of marketing research is to provide market-based insights and information to help guide effective business decisions. Kotler and other marketing gurus emphasize a problem-based approach to marketing generally and marketing research, specifically (Kotler and Keller, 2009). This translates into any other context for which one might consider using focus groups and depth interviews or, for that matter, other research methods.

Many consultants and research firms claim to have proprietary black-box techniques or methods that they will apply to your problem. Sometimes they have entire, pre-designed focus group or interview templates that they can take off the shelf, change a few labels and words, and sell to the next comer. After all, they are (or claim to be) the experts.

In my decided opinion, a technique-based approach simply will not hack it in applied or business research. Just because one has a first-class hammer, one cannot treat everything like a nail. Nor does a client saying "I want you to do some hammering for me" mean you should just pick up your hammer and set to work. That's strictly for amateurs.

The true professional fits the methodology to the business problem or decision that needs to be addressed. Sometimes focus groups are the right methodology, other times not. The same is true of depth interviews. You need to ask some questions before leaping ahead in order not to take your client with you off a cliff.

CHAPTER 3

Six Key Uses of Depth Research

As I see it, there are six key uses or roles for depth research. Only the first of these seems to be widely recognized by less sophisticated clients and even many practitioners, and is often positioned as the only proper use for this or other qualitative research.

■ Key Uses of Depth Methods

Exploration & Discovery (Preliminary Research	Digging into Quantitative Results (Follow-up Research)	Simulation of Real-World Response
Prototype & Usability Testing	Customer-Centered Crafting	Brainstorming & Creativity

Exploration & discovery (preliminary research)

Arguably, the traditional and most widespread use of depth methods (and other qualitative techniques) has been in the exploratory versus confirmatory stages of the research process. When beginning the research process, for example, depth methods may be brought together to gain an overall understanding of a market landscape, to learn the lay of the land, so to speak, to provide a foundation for what comes next. Focus groups (versus interviews) have probably been employed most often in the context of marketing research and other business research, but they are at least occasionally used as preliminary research in many other contexts.

We can and do use groups and interviews to gain insight into subjects' everyday lives and professional worlds, what they do, how they do it, and why. Sometimes this, on its own, meets the research objectives, for example, when a client is entering into a new market or new market category. We can use depth research, for example, to develop and understand qualitative segments among customers or decision makers, to explore differences between users and nonusers, to understand buying processes, or simply to float a trial balloon and see what response it gets.

However, the discovery role of depth research should not be thought of as just surveying and mapping new or changing markets, communities and stakeholders, social situations, policy challenges, or needs and issues. Because depth research allows for open-ended probing while keeping the flow of topics and issues on track, and also allowing the conversation to emerge as it will (versus following word-for-word a tightly structured and sequenced discussion guide), we can discover the unexpected and unanticipated. In my experience, this is particularly true for focus groups as peer-to-peer interaction can uncover material you would not know to ask about. That is, depth methods allow for serendipity — focus groups more so than individual interviews, as the interaction among group members can open up new lines of questioning based on their differing experience, knowledge, and practice.

It is an industry best practice to precede survey research with depth research, as my good friend and long-term client, David Harris argues in his excellent guide to developing questionnaires (Harris, 2014). He describes how preliminary qualitative research can not only inform surveys but get at factors that are simply not addressable quantitatively — not only the whys and hows, but also what people mean by the words they use. Furthermore, as is generally accepted, researchers have long used exploratory qualitative research to generate hypotheses, which then are operationalized and tested statistically.

More than that, this time-tested sequence can enable the researcher to maximize the value of survey research by understanding the market and market dynamics at a high level, learning the respondents' language/terminology, determining what types of questions are validly asked of them, what range of answers to expect, even how to ask the questions. At times a formal process known as "cognitive interviewing" is used for this purpose, typically done with individual interviews rather than groups. Similarly, one might use focus groups or interviews to help design quantitative exercises to optimize advanced statistical analyses, such as multiple trade-off methods (conjoint/discrete choice) where one presents respondents with a set of options to choose among.

Digging into quantitative results

Another use of focus groups, which is arguably (but only somewhat) more widely recognized than those that follow, is to go back and dig into the results of quantitative research. Most frequently, perhaps, "post-quant" focus groups are being used to dig into findings that seem puzzling or simply not well understood. In this capacity, one is really conducting a second round of exploratory qualitative research into a specific set of issues or as a means to understand better a specific set of responses.

Focus groups and depth interviews can also be used to illuminate the results of advanced statistical analyses, like segmentation, conjoint or discrete choice and other quasi-experimental tasks. For example, one can use groups to explore customer segments identified in formal survey research; to understand, in depth, segment members' motives (the "whys"), lifestyles, commonalities, and variations. In addition to deepening our understanding of such results, learnings from follow-up focus groups might then be used to develop heuristics (i.e., a scorecard) to classify prospective customers into a specific segment in order to target them for the most relevant promotional message or approach.

Similarly, one might use depth research to understand the whys behind the results of multiple trade-off analysis like conjoint and discrete choice where survey respondents are asked to identify their preferences for various product scenarios. Personally, I think focus groups provide a better context for this type of inquiry than individual interviews since they put those with differing viewpoints together and add that element of group interaction. For example, why did this group member indicate that they were most likely to opt for a conventional 20-cubic-foot, stainless steel refrigerator with French doors for $2,000 while another preferred a "smart" double-door refrigerator with otherwise similar features for $1,000 more? The data show us what they prefer, even the relative strength of preference (or dislike), but not the whys. How do they feel about these options? What benefits do they see them as providing?

Depth research can of course, be applied to exploring quantitative findings outside of marketing research. You might, for example, use focus groups or interviews in public policy or community studies to understand response segments or preferences for different program configurations.

In summary, it is possible to use depth research both as the lead-in to a quantitative study and post-quantitatively to explore outcomes. This type of qual-quant-qual design can maximize the value of a study. The exploratory qualitative portion helps the team to understand background issues in depth and to optimize the survey, both the research design and the actual instrument(s). Post-survey interviews or groups would then enable the team to understand findings in depth, perhaps also to craft or test possible next steps (such as strategies or tactics suggested by the quantitative results), better understand response segments, or follow-up on intriguing or unanticipated findings.

Simulation of real world response

A related use of depth research, focus groups especially, is *to simulate real-world responses* to situations, issues, products, strategies and concepts, advertisements, political candidates, you name it. Depth research can provide a context to obtain customer (or other target audience) feedback that offers a more realistic outcome than individual interviews. As I've suggested, a skillful moderator uses the power of peer-to-peer interaction to "keep it real."

By getting focus group members to question or challenge one another's presentations of self, the moderator can use group dynamics to prompt members to take off these social "masks" and reveal what they really think, feel, do, or are likely to do. Once you get the ball rolling, the moderator can get group members to test one another's and even their own statements and positions. That is, get them to halt the normal process of social posturing.

Such social psychological dynamics can provide a level of realism beyond what can be obtained through individual interviews, even quantitative surveys (with the possible exception of those using advanced analytics that uncover revealed importance and preferences). By encouraging the group members to feel that they are part of a community of peers, the adept moderator can get them to respond to questions and other stimuli with a level of realism that cannot otherwise be obtained. Of course, another part of the practitioner's job is to avoid "groupthink" or domination by one or a few group members, but this is always a necessary demand on the focus group practitioner.

This can be applied to virtually any research problem where one seeks to determine how people will respond to a specific type of situation or stimulus, and provides both insights and explicit suggestions for modifying or optimizing response. For instance, electricity outages are not only a problem for consumers and businesses that experience them, but their frequency and how customers are notified about their causes, what the utility is doing about them, and what to expect when they occur are a major source of dissatisfaction with electricity suppliers. I have conducted a number of groups for energy utilities to provide guidance regarding how best to communicate about power outages (e.g., their extent and duration) or how affected customers can find out such information (call, go online, text, etc.). How will customers respond to possible messages, ways of communicating about the outage — how can these things be optimized — and what options for learning more will best meet their needs and also maximize satisfaction or minimize anger and frustration with the energy provider?

Prototype and usability testing

You can also use depth methods as a vehicle for testing prototypes, websites and online tools, including for usability. While this can be accomplished in depth interviews, you can generally maximize value by combining individual responses with group discussion. This has traditionally been done via in-person groups. For example, one client was developing a new generation GPS device, so we conducted a series of groups in which consumers were given prototypes and encouraged to try out their features (this was followed by a series of "ride-along" field tests in which the prototypes were tested by asking each of a few group members to use the GPS to drive to an unfamiliar location). I've also done something similar with prototypes of new Valentine's Day candy prototypes, and with new surgical or medical devices. In one case, we discovered that the best way to explore new technology with surgeons was to develop a short video documenting the devices in actual use and showing this to groups of surgeons along with a few actual prototypes.

While this can be done with traditional groups, I have had excellent results exploring websites and online tools within the context of an online focus group. For example, promoting energy conservation is a statutory obligation of regulated utility companies in the United States. A major West Coast utility wanted to encourage its business customers to conserve electricity (and, incidentally, reduce their energy costs) by signing up for a new program in which they would conduct a "self-audit" of their firm's energy practices, obtain tips for conservation, and receive appropriately targeted offers for reduced-cost technology, more energy efficient equipment, and even zero-interest loans for energy upgrades. So I conducted a series of online focus groups with businesspeople who had signed up for the program but had not taken full advantage of its offerings. After discussion of relevant needs and issues, we went online to a live "test" version of the energy audit tool (a special website).

I then had one group member take control of the cursor and show us how she or he had navigated through the website, what they did (e.g., which "tabs" they had clicked on) and how they completed the questions, while providing a running narration regarding what they were thinking and experiencing. The rest of the group was able to observe and even comment silently by keyboarding into a "chat" box. Then I had a second person show us how they had used the site. After a few group members had done this, I had the group take a "guided tour" of the website and all of its contents, many features which virtually none of the group members had discovered or used on their own. For example, none had found their way to the part where they could obtain information and applications for interest-free energy upgrade loans. This process identified what users liked and disliked, uncovered navigation, content, and other issues, and provided direction to the client regarding how to improve usability, optimize wording, content, presentation (e.g., imagery, fonts, colors, placement) and encourage fuller use of their energy conservation offerings.

Brainstorming and creativity

Focused brainstorming and other creative thinking can be accomplished within either depth interview or focus group settings, although, once again, you can probably maximize the value of your research by leveraging group dynamics. There is a large body of literature on this topic, which was first popularized by a U.S. advertising executive, Alex F. Osborne (1953). My general recommendation is that the group setting is better for this purpose due to group dynamics. Brainstorming and other creative processes can be the primary purpose of a session, but are more often just one "module" within a larger framework. That is, the moderator facilitates a process in which group members are presented with a problem or topic and then guided to generate ideas, possibilities, or solutions. The basic idea is guiding group members to come up with ideas, without censoring them in any way, and to play off one another in doing so. After the flow of ideas runs down, one can also get them to "vote" on which should be considered "keepers," perhaps then brainstorm next steps.

Many additional and related techniques have been introduced over the years, with numerous useful references to be found online. For example, one can use focus groups as a context for co-creation (Ramawamy and Gouillart, 2010) in which one brings the group together to collaboratively design strategies, tactics, services, programs, or the like. This is a "hot" concept in the business world today that applies equally to the public, community, and other sectors. Using focus groups (in person or online) as the platform enables one to harness the creativity of stakeholders and, in particular, those who would be affected by or use the product or service in a way that best meets the needs and preferences of all involved. This is a kind of crowd-sourcing in miniature that can be the primary objective of a focus group, series of groups, or (as I have used it) as part of the overall qualitative research plan, typically done as a module within each of the groups.

Customer-Centered crafting

A less widely recognized use of focus groups is to harness group dynamics to help craft concepts and messages, even products; not just test or react to them. While depth interviews can also be used for customer-centered crafting, here too they don't give you that extra *je ne sais quoi.* The key idea is to use customer feedback to test and refine product or promotional concepts drafted by the manufacturer or advertising agency. Outside of marketing research, this might be described as participant-centered rather than customer-centered, but it's the same basic idea. One might explore anything from programs and paperwork to crafting the presentation of arguments and case elements to a jury (à la the TV program *Bull*). Such uses can include exposing the group to prototypes, storyboards, visual or media depictions of actual products, promotional concepts, or messages and using the group's feedback, with appropriate probing by the moderator, to critique and refine them. This is something that would be extremely difficult to accomplish using purely quantitative techniques, although it is certainly amenable to qualitative/quantitative hybrid methods.

Depth methods offer a very amenable context for projective techniques and other methods that can be harnessed for crafting concepts, products, brands, policies, programs and services. These can be just part of what goes on in a group or the primary focus of the session.

Projective techniques

Projective techniques are used to dig below the rational surface of how people think, feel about, and relate to virtually anything you wish to explore in this way. I will describe some techniques of this type below, but they are legion. There are actually two basic families of such techniques:

Reactive projective techniques

Reactive techniques start with presenting a stimulus of some kind — it may be a picture, an object, almost anything — and proceed by obtaining participants' responses to them. Normally you actually present a number of stimuli that vary in some way. For example, one research organization I worked with provided me with a deck of abstract paintings in different styles and colors. Then you ask each group member to choose the one that best fits how he or she thinks and feels about a particular product or whatever the group has been convened to explore.

Alternatively, you might show group members some stimuli which you have strategically selected and ask them what story they take away from it. For example, in a project where we were exploring how to interest middle school and high school women in STEM careers (science, technology, engineering and mathematics), we showed them pictures of various women who happened to be in such careers and asked them to tell us what story they got from the pictures, what type of person she was, and what she did for a living.

You can also employ reactive project methods with logos, branding graphics, whatever. In a recent employee study, for example, we showed a number of logos for firms in a variety of industries and asked group members to write down what they feel like or mean or represent to them, thinking of the design itself and not the actual company behind it. Or you can show a number of logos, branding, or similar concepts and ask group members to tell you what each is like for them, even to tell a story about it.

Constructive projective techniques

You can also do this the other way round — have participants draw or otherwise create an image or object that represents a product, brand, or other object of exploration during the session, how they feel about it, what it means to them, etc. One popular version of this is "collaging," having interviewees or group members create a collage with the same purpose. For example, you might hand out a bunch of magazines, scissors, glue and paper and ask them to go through the magazines, cut out images or words or other things they find there and assemble them into a collage that represents or feels like whatever you are exploring. Constructive exercises like this can be done as an individual or group activity or, as I have occasionally done, by break-out minigroups, who then present their work to the reassembled group as a whole.

Brainstorming

Most of us are familiar with brainstorming, at least to some degree. Basically, you get people — individually or together — to think up and, almost as stream-of-consciousness, come up with ideas, names, concepts, policies, products, programs, or solutions. You tell them not to censor but just blurt it out. Then, typically, one goes back and gets the group to vote on which works best, which they most like, and so on. There is a huge amount of literature on brainstorming. My point is that focus groups and, for some purposes, depth interviews provide an excellent setting within which to employ such techniques.

Co-creation exercises

Another approach is to have group members work together to assemble or craft a concept, product, policy, program, or approach that meets specifications you provide, fills a specific need, or offers a better alternative to what they currently have. This could also be a name, a logo, a symbol, a positioning, concept statement, even a mascot. Basically it is a mini-group-sourcing exercise in which you harness the creativity of group members to collaboratively craft "it" (whatever "it" is).

Gamification

Here, the method is to turn what you are asking participants to do into some manner of game or add game-like elements. A hot topic since about 2010, gamification has been integrated into marketing, work situations, other business areas, education, or technology design. There is an enormous amount of literature on this topic, although much of it (like the very concept itself, apparently) tends to be produced by entrepreneurs and companies offering gamification services, consulting, even software. Customer-centered crafting and even engagement in other activities can be enhanced by incorporating elements of gamification in focus group exercises. With a little imagination, you could also apply this concept to individual interviews. My point here is simply that elements of gamification can be employed within depth research to increase participant engagement, harness both their cooperative and competitive proclivities, and leverage the sense of play toward the goals of your project.

PART 2

DEPTH RESEARCH PLANNING AND PREPARATION FOR HIGH IMPACT

CHAPTER 4

Key Steps in Planning Depth Research

Remember the client who says "I want some focus groups" or "I want some interviews"? Where do you go from there? Doing depth research is much like painting a house, in that careful preparation and planning are essential to a successful result. And, as for house painting, once you have put in that "prep" time, the actual job of doing the research will go smoothly and relatively quickly, at least until Murphy's Law tosses a pie in your face, which will happen when you least expect it, and you have to improvise a workaround. As always, "the devil is in the details."

Seasoned professionals make it look easy, effortless even, but even they need to take the time and put in the work to craft the optimal design. And I use the word "craft" intentionally. Actionable research design is not a science. It's not something you can mass produce on some kind of assembly line. Nor can you just take a standardized solution off the shelf or out of your computer file, and apply it like an all-purpose black box. You've got needs, goals, tools, and constraints within which you have to work. At the very least, you have to tweak what you've done previously, thinking through every aspect to meet the specific needs and goals of each project.

Four + One questions

Your first step should be to map out the situation (literally or not, as works best for you) and determine precisely what needs to be done, including whether or not depth methods are the right approach to meet a client's needs, regardless of whether the requestor thinks they have given you enough information to design and bid the research. Fortunately, designing the right approach to meeting client needs relies on using one of the researcher's main strengths: asking questions. There are four key questions to probe and an additional question that will help you deal with the internal or external clients asking about most any potential application of depth methods.

■ 4+1 Key Design Questions

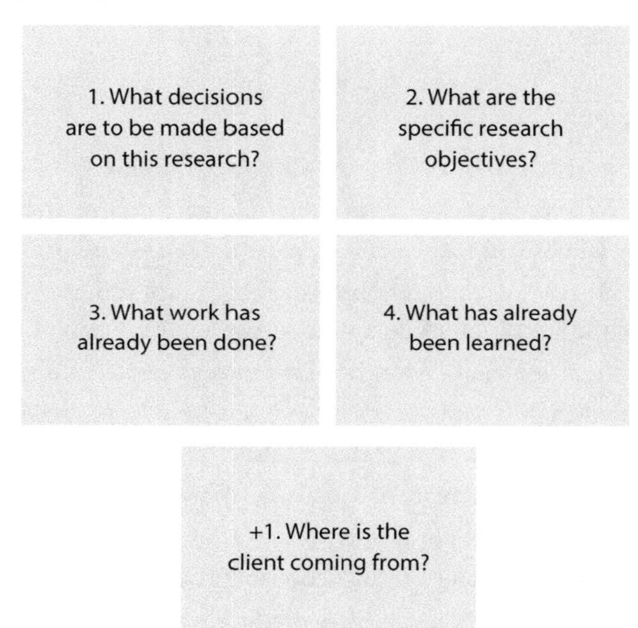

What are the underlying decisions to be made based on this research?

The research plan, including your methodology, should be purpose-designed to address specific business, organizational, or other needs, challenges, and problems. As Harris (2014) suggests, this starts with identifying the business, organizational, or other relevant decisions that are to be made based on the research. If these things are not clearly spelled out in the request for proposal (RFP) or equivalent (e.g., an email request or conversation), you need to probe and tease them out. Usually there are no second-chances with respect to launching a product or program or meeting emergent challenges in other contexts.

What are the specific research objectives?

Often, but not always — at least in marketing research — the request for proposal or equivalent will lay out specific strategic and tactical objectives for the research, ideally in addition to the decisions that the research is to inform and support. If anything, defining and understanding these research objectives is even more important than scoping out the decisions to be made or actions to be taken based on the study. They are more immediate and, from the researcher's pragmatic angle, even more crucial to satisfying your client who may or may not be personally involved in subsequent steps and their results. So, if you are not clear about your client's concrete research objectives, eliciting them is mission-critical.

All too often, RFPs are vaguely written or the research need has not been clearly, or at least adequately, thought through and defined. Even if objectives are provided, even at risk of annoying the client, the researcher may be well advised to get back to the originator and probe to understand them better. Sometimes it is necessary to push back a bit or at least sort out which objectives can be met with focus groups or depth interviews, another methodology, a combined research program, or met at all. Often the requestor literally "throws in the kitchen sink" when asking for a project and assumes they can get from it more than a single study or even multi-phased project can support. At other times, they may not have adequately thought through their objectives or they may have left out relevant objectives that can be met with the same design and provide added value. Sometimes they are just passing along a request from an internal client, who, yes, just asked for "some interviews or focus groups."

What work has already been done?

Another key consideration is what has already been done — what steps have already been taken, such as prior primary or secondary research, test marketing, internal workshopping or deliberations, SWOT analyses, competitive intelligence, and so forth? Clients may want to keep much of this secret — sometimes even after they award the job — perhaps even as a kind of test for the potential research supplier. Nevertheless, asking and knowing about what has already been done or tried is important to crafting the right research plan (and looking smart).

What has already been learned?

Closely related, and sometimes even harder to pry loose from the requester, is understanding what has already been learned. Almost nothing makes a proposal or the researcher look more inept than promising to find out what the client already knows, or, worse, implying that something they have already found out isn't so and needs to be researched (even if that is the reality — in which case you need to tread delicately). You want to design a plan to extend what is known or qualitatively test assumptions, even prior findings in order to confirm or reject them. The goal is to dig deeper or more broadly or more strategically than has already been done, not to go over the same ground again (unless there is a known problem with the prior methodology or findings).

Where is the client coming from?

The four basic questions lead to a related pragmatic question for the researcher — understanding where that client is coming from. You need to work with them and obtain their buy-in to avoid the possibility of working at cross-purposes. First, you need to uncover the requestor's (and their team's) biases, which are not typically made explicit unless you — subtly — probe. In recent years, for example, focus groups have fallen out of favor in many industries, sometimes in favor of interviews, sometimes in favor of asynchronous, online, behavioral or "high tech" methods like brain scans or proprietary black-box techniques. This may be due in part to fad, in part to poorly moderated focus groups that have turned people against the method, and in part to all the competing claims and directives argued in marketing books and articles, or reliance on "big data" such as that which may be captured at point of sale for retail products or by online tools counting numbers of hits, click-throughs, purchases, etc. The same goes for depth interviews, although they seem to be less subject to cyclic ups and downs. Unless you find out about and address these biases — and do not try to push a research design that clients will reject — you're setting yourself up to run into any number of problems, not the least of which is not being hired to do the research.

Similarly, it is important to elicit precisely what the requestor and their team expects. Such considerations are probably more often unstated than explicit, more likely to be taken for-granted until or unless they are not met. You may need to directly address and negotiate expectations. These may range from something as trivial as the kind of food to serve focus group observers, to expectations regarding what they can get out of the research process itself, how the researcher will dress or speak, how they will run the sessions, to which issues are most important in the discussion guide, "need to knows," and which are merely "nice to know."

This last item ties into ascertaining what and how much the client and their team actually know. How knowledgeable are they about qualitative methodology? Do they really understand what their options are and what they can get from depth methods? Are their expectations realistic? Do they have a reasonable idea of how to use appropriately the results of focus groups or depth interviews? Obviously, such issues need to be handled delicately, but you can set yourself up for disaster if there is a significant gap between what the requestors know (or think they know) and what they need to know to make a sound decision about the research and how to go about it.

Secondly, you need to find out what the requestor actually knows about the substantive issues associated with the research problem, products, category, market, organizational or social context, consumer behavior and so forth. One the one hand, clients may rely on the researcher to provide guidance on these issues or to design exploratory research to, among other things, shed light on them. On the other, they may feel strongly that they are the content experts, that they know what they need and want, and that the researcher shouldn't raise any questions or offer any suggestions. This is more often the case when the researcher is hired only to moderate the groups, but, even then, gentle probing can help greatly in understanding where there might be gaps that the research can fill in.

Systematic depth research design

Okay, you have enough information to move forward with a depth solution for your client's needs. Based on my experience designing and doing groups and interviews, consider this a systematic approach to doing so.

■ Systematic Depth Research Design

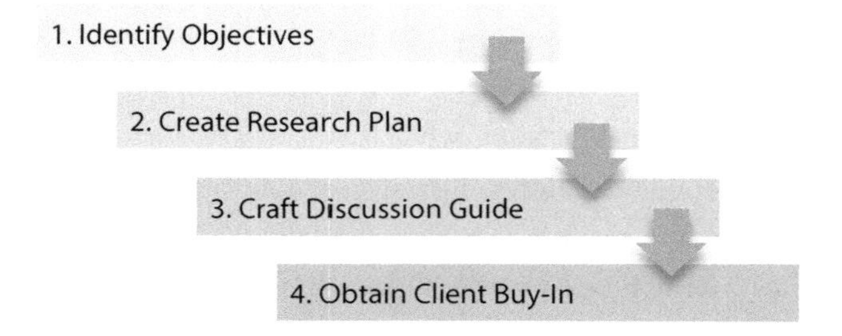

Identifying the objectives

Your first step is to spec out the objectives of the research. As noted above, the process typically starts with some kind of RFP from an internal or external client, which will generally detail the underlying business such as organizational, institutional, or community. and its challenges, problems, decisions, or issues underlying the request. The RFP may provide a more or less well-thought-out statement of the requestor's objectives for the research. Whether or not you have the benefit of such a starting point, I and other seasoned researchers will tease these out and break them down into specific objectives.

I strongly suggest that you consciously *operationalize* the project objectives. However fuzzy or aspirational the objectives are as presented by the client or project team (including yourself), define it in a way that is clear, *measurable* and subject to empirical observation, at least to the extent that one can determine if the objective has or has not been satisfied. We are not using this term in its strictest scientific sense, but rather making goals and objectives tangible, concrete — ideally something you can go back to and check to see if they were met.

Example of four operational objectives for product or service research:

- **Explore what today's customers need and want from products/ services of this type**
- **Understand their experiences with, attitudes regarding, and perceptions of key competitors/alternatives**
- **Evaluate their responses to the new product/service concept**
- **Test the proposed messaging and establish how to optimize it to maximize purchase consideration**

Notice that these, while generic for our purposes here, are all focused and action-oriented. Outside of marketing research, for example policy research or other applied work, these objectives would be adapted to that situation. In any case, they effectively constitute the researcher's "marching orders" and help you determine the right methodology to meet the client's objectives.

Now, let me provide an overview of next steps as the following chapters will be devoted to the detailed work leading up to actually doing your groups or interviews.

Creating the research plan

Now you are ready to determine the best approach to meet these operational objectives. Let's assume that depth methods would be optimal or at least suitable. Your first challenge is to put together a preliminary research plan based on the project objectives and what you already know about the topics, the client, background, and methodology. In professional practice, your typical next step is to work up a proposal, outlining those objectives, fleshing out your research plan, explaining details, timing, cost and whatever else is required to obtain approval. On authorization to proceed, you then go back, refine, update or revise the research plan based on client feedback as part of the project kick-off.

Doing the needful

Once you have an approved project and research design, you (or your team members) have to finalize a workplan and do whatever is needed to implement it. If you're lucky, most of this can be done by others — many organizations have field and operations units that will take care of what I personally consider the boring logistical details. Sometimes the burden is on you. In any case, you have to set up the research and deal with clients and their bureaucracies. You or your team has to find and reserve research facilities or locations, organize recruitment, staffing, invoicing, recording, transcripts, getting yourself and clients to the sessions, perhaps flight or train and hotel reservations, often up-front payments for services — myriad logistical details. We'll cover some of these, but by no means all as, while absolutely necessary, they are peripheral to doing the actual research.

Very commonly, there will be lots of starts and stops. Clients will change their objectives, redefine target audiences, produce and change materials, ask for schedule changes. Client team structure and players will change. There will be recruiting problems and all manner of challenges.

Expect stuff to happen; don't be surprised. Murphy's Law ("whatever can go wrong, will go wrong") is a fact of life for the depth researcher. Deal with it. Keep your sense of humor about you. Be flexible, but be firm and stand by what you believe is important or essential. I can't emphasize this enough.

Obtaining client buy-in

Let's go back to, "client buy-in." Something textbooks don't tell you, and I want to make clear from the start, is that it is critical to obtain client buy-in to the research plan, to its major components and functional details. Often they, in turn, need to obtain buy-in from their internal clients, colleagues, superiors, and, increasingly often, financial gatekeepers.

Clients vary in how engaged they get in the details of research beyond accepting the initial proposal. You need to know your client and manage the situation appropriately. For example, multiple (sometimes energizing and sometimes frustrating) meetings or teleconferences are required. Doing things the client wants "their way," even if that seems counterproductive to you, such as writing extremely explicit or specifically structured discussion guides that you will probably not be able to follow.

You may need to make trade-offs between what you believe is the best way to go and what clients will accept, or get them to make trade-offs between all their "wants" so they can get what they need from the research. You may spend a lot of time explaining:

- Specific recommendations
- Your proposed methodology
- The relative benefits of the suggested methodology and alternative approaches
- How you will do specific tasks
- What observers should expect to see and hear
- What can and cannot be done, and why
- How the client(s) can help make it all work
- What they should and should not do, including expected decorum during research. Clients can surprise you. During one depth interview project, my clients started shooting spitballs at the one-way mirror!

One thing to avoid is coming off like a "professor," or standing on your status as a professional researcher. While I must admit (and you may have noticed) that I personally tend to fall into that quagmire unless I proceed very deliberately and self-consciously, as many of us have learned from experience, this creates struggles you cannot win and simply wastes everyone's time.

Once you have buy-in, you're pretty much home free, as long as you execute what you promised in a manner satisfactory to the client. Without a client's full buy-in, you are treading on very treacherous ground indeed. No matter how exemplary your research plan, execution, and analysis, you are likely to find yourself in lose-lose situations.

A note on project team continuity

For the remainder of this book, I will speak of the "project team" to include clients, colleagues, and any other stakeholders (besides the moderator) who are involved in the depth research. These can include others in the client firm or organization than just your immediate contacts, including their internal clients and more senior management, advertising or public relations staff, consultants, boards, marketing partners, agency staff, officials, or your own colleagues.

Little is more counterproductive than having team members show up somewhere in midstream, not knowing what has gone before, and start trying to second guess or tinker with the research. Time and again, someone new shows up with a different agenda, a different take on the research objectives and how they should be met. Or they are uninformed, regarding what has gone on before, been agreed upon or learned, the research plan or methodologies. In a worst-case situation, you discover battling factions each with their own assumptions, objectives, demands and expectations popping in and out of the client team.

To the extent that they will be actively involved in monitoring the sessions, developing or modifying materials, making decisions based on the results, or wish to be part of the research process, it is optimal for your core client team members to become and remain actively involved throughout the project, if only to create buy-in to the results.

In particular, those who will be involved in making on-the-spot decisions regarding methodology, process, or stimulus materials should attend all or most events — in person if it's in-person research. Realistically, they can keep involved through video-streaming or video-conferencing. The key is maximizing continuity of the project team and its involvement in the ongoing process.

CHAPTER 5

Physical Set-Up of Depth Research

Let's skip ahead to something tangible — the set-up. Understanding and visualizing the physical context of in-person or online focus groups will help you plan how you can best conduct them. At the end of the chapter, we'll cover how this can be adapted for depth interviews.

In-Person focus group set-up

It is the norm for today's commercial depth research facilities to offer specially designed focus group suites, commonly several of these to allow a number of groups to be conducted simultaneously. When a person arrives at the facility, there is some kind of waiting room, occasionally seating areas set aside for members of each group or interview. Participants check in, may be asked to complete a "re-screener" to ensure that they have the right profile, or possibly to fill out some pre-session exercises or other paperwork (e.g., a release for use of their information and image). When the moderator is ready, group members are ushered into the actual focus group suite. It is helpful to visualize the physical set-up. A modern focus group suite in a professional qualitative research facility is typically set up something like that shown in the figure below:

■ Example of focus group set up

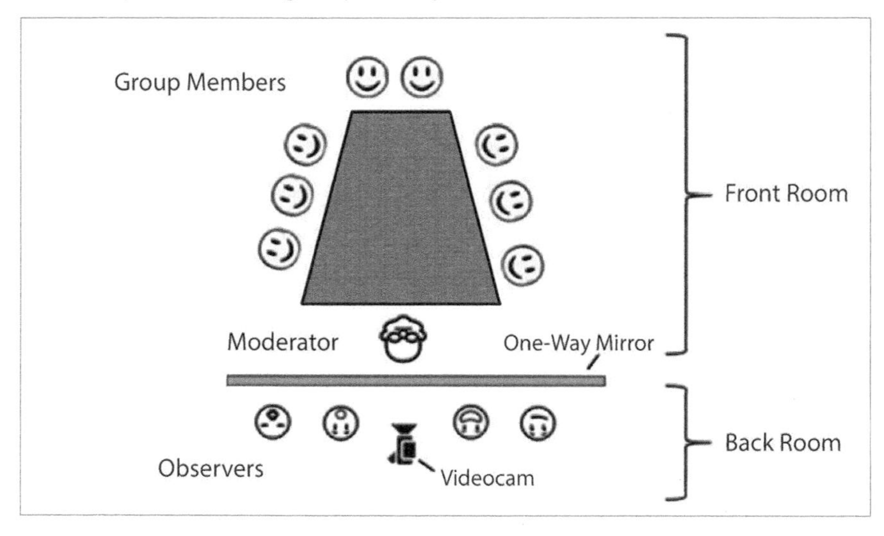

The focus group members and moderator sit around a table in a brightly lit "front room" or "focus group room." The trapezoidal table shape shown is actually the best design. Pop quiz: why do I say that?

Although I was initially confused when a research company I worked for installed one of these in our own, internal focus group room, wondering why the moderator would sit alone at the wide end, it was pointed out to me that this table shape allows the moderator, observers and video camera to see all the group members' faces.

Despite that benefit, it seems that most facilities continue to provide rectangular tables or "U" shaped set-ups. It is common for several tables to be pushed together. These are undoubtedly cheaper than purpose-built trapezoidal tables, and they work pretty well. What you don't want is a round table as that places some participants with their backs to the moderator and observers. A round table may also implicitly reduce the status of the moderator from "director" of the event to one among equals, which, to my mind, would be problematic.

Sensitive microphones often hang from the ceiling of the front room. Typically, there are flip charts to write on, sometimes white boards for that purpose; some way to hang visual materials on the walls or place them on a ledge; computers or other technology for the participants' or moderator's use if the research design calls for that; monitors to watch stimuli on screen or an actual projection screen and video projector hooked up to a laptop; and beverages to drink. In Europe wine and beer are often served to group members, but I have never seen this done in the U.S., although quite a few facilities have wine and beer available for the team in the back room. A few rooms may provide more advanced technology, like white boards that will copy and reproduce what is written on them.

The focus group room is separated from the back room by a one-way mirror, with the back room lighting kept low enough that group members cannot see through the mirror. This set-up was, incidentally, pioneered by National Analysts when they developed an in-house facility over 50 years ago and has become standard for dedicated focus group research centers in the U.S. This is far, far preferable to having observers sitting in the same room as focus group members, less cumbersome and subject to glitches than using some kind of video link to allow attending clients and other team members to observe.

Clients, note-takers, and other observers normally sit in the back room and attend to the proceedings. On occasion, (to be realistic, all too often and too loudly), observers will get involved in conversations or discussions, go online with their computer or smartphone and check e-mail or conduct other business. It's only prudent to remind your observers to keep any conversations low enough so that they cannot be heard in the front room and to avoid turning on lights or even turning laptop screens toward the one-way mirror, as that may not only remind group members that they are being observed (something you always tell them but want them to forget about and attend to the moderator and fellow group members), but also let them see into the back room as it is the difference in light levels that makes the one-way mirror one-way.

Typically, in the back room and additional client lounges, there will be a variety of snacks and beverages available, and meals will be served at dinnertime. Focus group researchers and clients like to joke about gaining weight from eating all those M&Ms. There are usually desks or ledges to sit behind and take notes or place one's laptop on, comfortable sofas, and other amenities. Modern facilities typically provide wireless internet access, electrical and/or USB plug-ins. Although some facilities continue to cook meals for clients and group members — there is one in the Baltimore, Maryland area that, last I heard, still makes their own amazing crab cakes — it has become the norm for facilities to assemble menus from local restaurants (typically with prices blanked out) and ask the back room to order from these early in the evening for delivery at a later time.

There is usually a video camera or more advanced video-taping or video-conferencing system, commonly "behind the mirror." Video-conferencing allows the group to be observed remotely by streaming image and sound directly to team members' home or office computers. Some new technologies allow a 360° recording of the group and let you mark sections of particular interest. Speakers in the back room allow everyone in attendance to listen to the group. There are often additional monitors in client lounges and other areas where clients might gather outside of the back room.

CDRs, DVDs and/or MP3 recordings are usually made and provided to the clients as well as the researchers, or else an audio or audiovisual recording may be created and made available for remote downloading. If the group is conducted in a language different from that of the observers, clients or research team, there is typically a simultaneous translator present in the back room, whose narrative is recorded. Special multi-channel equipment is usually provided to facilitate listening to and recording both the original and the simultaneous translation.

While, as described above, the majority of groups in such facilities are conducted around a table of some configuration, facilities may offer alternatives such as "living room" set-ups or theater-type rows of seats. The former design is obvious intended to create an informal atmosphere and maximize participant comfort, but I have not personally used that configuration. Theater-type seating, in contrast, may facilitate observing presentations or videos, but seems to implicitly define participants as "audience members," promote serial interviewing and discourage crystallization of a group or group dynamics. Yet another variant is for the facility to have a "test kitchen" that can be used for studies in which participants prepare some type of food and might be interviewed while they do so, or even prompted to facilitate in group discussion, although much of the "action" would probably take place in a later module of the session around a focus-group table.

Online focus group set-up

Let's use "platform" to describe how online focus groups are set up on the computer screen, the virtual analog of a physical focus group suite. There are no hard and fast rules governing the set-up of an online focus group platform and, in fact, as digital technology continues to evolve, we can expect new forms and variations to emerge. So let's focus on what is available today and, specifically, the type of platform I am accustomed to working with.

From what I have been able to ascertain, most (if not all) of the currently available webcam-enabled online focus group platforms are built on the same underlying software, Adobe Connect. This system essentially provides a website that can be divided into a number of "pods" or windows, the size and location of which can be modified pretty much at will. However, there is a basic functional design that essentially replicates and extends the typical focus group suite but, of course, virtually. Here is a simplified example:

■ Example of Online Groups Platform (Moderator's View)

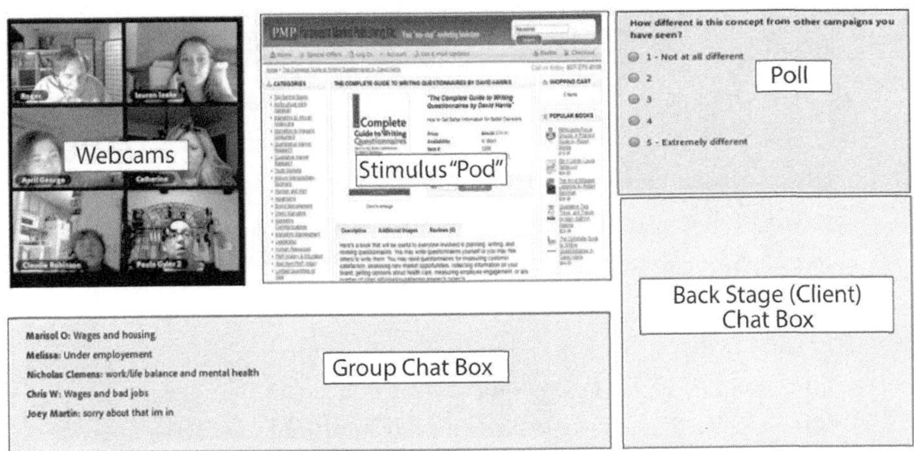

Let's examine the "pods" shown above.

Webcams

You can see what some of my colleagues call a "Brady Bunch" group of webcam thumbnails on the upper left, with the focus group participants and moderator (that's me, with the headphones, probably looking at my discussion guide). Actually, this pod with the individual thumbnails can be expanded or contracted as needed. For example, in a recent project, the client team wanted to be able to use participants' faces and show their facial expressions in their educational and marketing materials, so we expanded this pod whenever screen "real estate" was not being actively used by another pod.

Real estate and visibility also tend to impose a practical limit on the number of focus group members. Although I have done groups with up to 10 or 12 members, the optimal number for good visibility without taking up too much of the screen has proven to be six to eight individuals (plus the moderator). More than that, the thumbnails become so small as to be hard to "read."

Although focus group members can (and do sometimes) participate without a webcam, it is optimal for each person to use a webcam and have his or her image up on the screen. This maximizes the sense of virtual reality, allows us to see and evaluate facial expressions and gestures, and generally maximizes the sense of being there in person. Sometimes a group member will refuse to use a webcam, may not have or know how to use one, although we may supply a webcam to those without one as part of the incentive. A participant's webcam may not work, or there may be some kind of glitch so that their image does not appear. While far from optimal, these represent some of the eventualities the adept moderator deals with if and when they occur.

Stimulus pod

This is one of the most useful features of an online groups platform. It allows you to show virtually any kind of stimulus — text, graphics, a PowerPoint presentation, video, audio track, or, as in the hypothetical illustration above, a web page. The system will let you play a video or go to a "live" website. I have, for example, used this facility in a number of groups where we go to and explore a website or online tool in real time within the stimulus pod, which can, of course, be expanded for visibility and ease of use. There is a feature in Adobe Connect that lets you release the cursor to a group member, so that she or he can navigate through a website, click on tabs, or use any tools, while the other group members observe. You can then give the cursor to another group member and let them go onto the website, or you can just navigate through the website to give group members a "guided tour."

Although not shown here, many platforms let you use a "whiteboard" pod or make whiteboard tools available, so that group members can mark up whatever is in the stimulus pod: for example, each person using a different color, or using one color to show what they like and another dislikes. Some platforms incorporate tools that allow group members to indicate their interest or liking for a video or audio track as it plays, and allow them to put up virtual "post-its."

Poll pod

Adobe Connect allows you to create and deploy survey-like numeric polls as well as short-answer questions. Basically, while functionality may be limited compared to what you can do with an online quantitative survey, you can create as many polls as you'd like in advance and pop them up on the screen at the appropriate time, not just in the location shown but anywhere you'd like. The software automatically tallies and shows the number or percentage of responses for each answer category. This panel (also shown in the platform example above) is an actual numeric poll used in one of my online group projects:

How different is this concept from other campaigns you have seen?

- ❍ 1 - Not at all different
- ❍ 2
- ❍ 3
- ❍ 4
- ❍ 5 - Extremely different

You can, alternatively, use short-answer questions asking group members to individually keyboard in their response. It functions the same way, with the same options as the numeric poll. As you can imagine, this is a very powerful tool that offers advantages beyond what is available from the in-person setting.

Another important feature is that, with Adobe Connect, group members only see their own responses onscreen. The moderator can click on a "broadcast" button, which then shows a summary of results — the number and percent of participants selecting each option or all the short-answers provided, but without identifying who said what. This is critically important in depth research as it keeps individual responses anonymous and focuses attention on the pattern of response. There is also another button that allows you (and observers in the virtual back room) to see who gave which answer. I often use this so I can probe responses, "Bill and Janet, you both chose 5, extremely different. Tell me about it . . ." Or "Two of you chose 1, 'not at all different,' please explain your reasoning."

Group chat box

This is essentially a conventional chat box into which any group member or the moderator can keyboard, providing a valuable supplement to the oral discussion that everyone is hearing. Because it's visible to everyone, this is not a good place for entering private, individual responses but still can be used to allow group members to keyboard in thoughts or answers to non-sensitive questions. Another use is allowing participants to enter or expand upon their responses while someone else is speaking. Some younger focus group members may be prone to keyboard rather than speak, which is something the moderator may need to call out, emphasizing that we principally want oral discussion.

Backstage chat box

This is another very cool feature, in effect simulating the "back room" in a physical focus group suite. It is a private chat box only visible to those who have been given what Adobe Connect terms "presenter" or "host" status. It allows team members to keyboard messages to one another and to the moderator, in effect, replacing the usual practice of passing notes into the focus group room. I have sometimes completely restructured a focus group based on what a client and I have keyboarded back and forth in this pod. Again, a moderator needs to be flexible!

There can be many variations on what we have explored here, and I have not shown other pods that can be used, such as an "attendance" pod that shows who is online and also indicates who is speaking at any single moment. There are additional tools that can be added, including the ability to create breakout rooms. Everything can be recorded in the virtual equivalent of a DVD and subsequently downloaded, including the sound track.

Voice Over Internet Protocol (VOIP)

It would be great to use the VOIP (Voice Over Internet Protocol) feature offered by many platforms you might employ for online or telephone research. Recruits and project team members often ask about this, but there are major issues given today's technology.

The most critical in my experience has been the bandwidth problem. When, for example, using Adobe Connect-based platforms my experience has been that taking advantage of built-in VOIP takes up too much "bandwidth." Everything else slows to a crawl or just stops working. Once in a while one of my online group participants or team members has used a VOIP connection but generally it is best to have them use a landline or mobile phone separate from the software platform you may be using. Call out to their phones or have them call in with their phones, even if using a video or audio conferencing platform, although this may become less of an issue as the technology continues to improve. So far, for me, the primary exception to this rule has been the rare occasion when I put on a headset plugged into my computer and use my company's phone management system, but even then, the project team and respondents almost always use a landline or mobile phones.

My intention has been to give readers a graphic understanding of what an online group platform looks like and some of the ways you can utilize its built-in capabilities. Personally, I have come to prefer this format whenever feasible and appropriate because it allows me to do more, more easily than is the case with in-person groups, to assemble cross-geography groups, and to avoid the time and hassle of travel for everyone.

Telephones & cell phones

In both the telephone and online modes of depth research, unless you are using VOIP, everybody uses a telephone or mobile phone. Your primary options today are to use a landline (or equivalent) or a mobile phone and to have participants and the client team do the same. That seems simple, but, like all seemingly simple things, you need to pay attention to the details. Phone problems can land you in a world of pain, or at least embarrassment and even mission-critical problems.

Few of us today continue to use corded landline phones or the equivalent. If not using a true mobile device, like a smartphone, we most often use cordless handsets. These generally work perfectly well, as long as your battery is charged. If you run out of battery (power), you might as well have a brick in your hand.

After a few embarrassing situations, I purchased a system for my home office that has a corded base unit and any number of cordless extension handsets. I normally do online groups and interviews or TDIs (and would do telephone focus groups) from my work desk, with my computer monitor before me and room for notepads, discussion guides, and so forth on the desk between the screen and my chair. I find it too clumsy to hold the handset while doing sessions, so I use a headset with both earphones and a microphone that plugs into my cordless handset. That generally works fine. I also have the base unit in front of me, slightly to the side of my monitor screen, so, if the cordless set's battery runs low, I can then switch to the corded handset with nobody the wiser.

Mobile phones are, obviously, an option for the moderator and participants alike. It is very likely that, whether you are doing a focus group or a depth interview, your respondents and clients will be using a smartphone.

While I still prefer a cordless phone with headset, I am increasingly using my smartphone for interviews and online groups although, I must admit, I am a bit hesitant about the microphone quality and unsure how to place the smartphone to maximize that.

Regardless of the type of phone, there are a number of issues to be aware of when you or others are using mobile phones (or even tablets, like iPads, that have telephone capabilities), or even if using cordless handsets:

Environment issues

In today's world of smartphones, tablets, and occasional older cellphones, it is particularly important to ensure that the interviewee or focus group member can participate from a quiet, safe and private location. Some will try to do interviews in public spaces or even while driving. Just as when doing telephone or online surveys, they should not be driving, operating machinery, or doing anything else that would be dangerous, distracting, or disruptive. You can't prevent dogs from barking or children from going to their parent (in fact, I will generally tell parents that it's okay for their kid to be there, unless they are being too noisy or distracting), but it's important to control participants' environment to the extent possible.

In virtually all cases you need any observers to be muted during the call. This is important. You can ask them to mute their devices or, if you are using an appropriate online platform, you can mute them from your end. You can all unmute and speak after or between sessions, but during a depth interview or focus group it is essential that neither you nor your research subjects hear the observers. Furthermore, open lines can create echo effects, introduce environmental noise, and otherwise disrupt the session.

The problem of speakerphones

While using a speakerphone on a landline or mobile phone is an option, not only do speakerphones tend to have inferior sound but they pick up environmental noise, typing sounds, and often create an echo effect that can be very disruptive. It is advisable to discourage interviewees (and focus group members) using mobile or landline phones from using a speaker-phone. They cause too many problems. So, when it comes to using speaker-phones in depth research, telephone or online, it's best to follow the simple principle: don't.

Battery issues

That brings me to another important tip relevant to any depth research in which smartphones or cordless handsets are used: be proactive in heading off battery problems. It should be you or your team's routine to caution interviewees and colleagues to start with a full battery and have an alternative device available to which they can switch, or else to use a corded landline. Time and again, I've had sessions disrupted when interviewees' or group members' phones run out of charge and they have to find another, often requiring them to hang up and call back into the session. It's not only problematic and disruptive but embarrassing.

Screen size issues

Obviously, the screens on mobile devices are smaller than those of desktop, laptop or notebook computers. This is not a problem for telephone interviews or groups, unless you, team members or group members need to see or read something on the screen. It is best not to rely on smartphones or smaller tablets for displaying graphics, or doing polls during online groups. I have had online group participants use tablets, and at least larger tablets have worked perfectly well, although I think everyone would have a better experience using a larger screen. That's not always feasible, however.

I personally use an extra-large monitor for online groups and interviews, although my primary computer these days is a laptop, which I plug into the monitor. If you'll be doing many online groups or interviews, I recommend using a large monitor or screen. I usually use my 21-inch monitor but have occasionally used my wife's 24-inch iMac, which is even nicer. You can use a smaller monitor or even laptop/notebook's native screen, but that makes it difficult to read small print onscreen. Obviously, I don't recommend trying to run online groups or depth interviews involving seeing or reading anything (including back-room chat) through a tablet, even if group members or clients use one.

Audio-recording the session

Normally, you arrange some method of recording both sides of the conversation and possibly make arrangements for clients to listen in to at least some of the calls. There are a number of professional services that can help with this, ranging from groups that will recruit, record, set up and bring you into the call to online services like Spiderphone, that allow you to call out to the interviewee, record the call and allow clients to monitor the interview. There are also digital devices and enterprise systems that can allow you to do this, possibly even software on your mobile phone. If you are videostreaming through a commercial service like FocusVision, recordings may be part of the standard deliverables.

Depth Interviews: set-up variations

For in-person IDIs all you really need are a couple of chairs, ideally with a small table between them, and means to record the session, either audio only or audiovisual. If client team members wish to observe, it is ideal to have a separate back room or equivalent. Central location facilities commonly use focus group rooms for depth interviews or have some "interview rooms" with smaller tables but otherwise set up the same way as focus group suites with a one-way mirror, client back room, and hosting.

For TDIs, I used to rely on a third-party audioconferencing platform that allows recording and client monitoring. These typically offer utilities that will call out to the interviewee or allow them to call in and join the call.

Recently, I have been using the same Adobe Connect-based platform for teleconferences that I use for online focus groups, generally without turning on webcams. When used this way, the process from the interviewee's perspective is exactly the same as for other TDIs. One major benefit is that the project team cannot only listen in to the interview and, as appropriate, see the platform screen but, and this is the key benefit, they use Backroom Chat to communicate with one another and the moderator via keyboarding. That has really opened up the interviews, allowing me and the project team to refine lines of questioning, respond to requests for clarification or legitimate interviewee questions on the fly. In short, this approach has been working out very well for me.

Visuals

Sometimes you need to show something to the interviewees such as a text concept or profile, PowerPoint slides, a video, even a website. While not an issue when doing in-person interviews with the appropriate technology, this is obviously problematic when you are doing the interview by phone. You could mail, FedEx, or email materials to them and trust that they will not jump ahead and read or review them before the interview (unless that is your intention). I've done that, but you have minimal control. I've found it preferable to use digital technology alongside the telephone to show visual and multimedia stimuli online while conducting the phone interview. Most commercial and enterprise conferencing services can arrange this.

Alternatively, the same platforms you might employ for online focus groups can also be used for what I have taken to calling "online depth interviews" (ODIs) allowing you to present visual or multimedia stimuli and record everything seen and heard during the interview. I have been using such a system for a while, even when not sharing visuals, normally without webcams but allowing the project team to observe and communicate through the virtual backroom. From the interviewee's viewpoint this is essentially the same as any telephone depth interview. In one study, I had the interviewees on a webcam so that we could document and observe them as they opened a test mail piece, both to ensure that they only did so at the appropriate time and also to see their facial expressions as they read the piece. We were able to then show and discuss the mailing. However, most of the time, I don't use webcams when doing ODIs.

CHAPTER 6

Four Depth Research Formats

Now that you have a better idea of what the physical context is within which you will work, let's go back to the pragmatics of designing the research. You've already worked out the objectives and decided that focus groups or depth interviews are the way to go for your project. Now you need to start on your detailed research plan. After enough time doing depth research, a lot of these steps are virtually simultaneous, but let's begin with deciding the format for conducting the sessions, of which there are four main alternatives:

1. In-person, using a professional focus group facility
2. In-person, using an alternative venue
3. By telephone
4. Online, using a videoconferencing or purpose-built platform

Let's consider each of these options in turn.

In-Person, using a professional focus group facility

The traditional and still most common approach in marketing research and many other commercial settings (e.g., mock juries) is conducting in-person, face-to-face groups or interviews in a dedicated central location facility. One-on-one depth interviews are often referred to as Individual Depth Interviews for which the conventional acronym is IDI.

Most commercial depth research in the U.S. today is conducted in dedicated research facilities that, in addition to one or more specially designed group or interview suites, provide recruiting and hosting services, and arrange for participant and observer meals. Some educational institutions, consultancies, or organizations may offer dedicated research suites as well.

Central location facilities today compete for being deluxe, contemporary, comfortable yet high-tech in design, with WiFi, and a full complement of uniformed and very professional hosting staff. While there are still quite a few excellent independent facilities, research facilities are increasingly part of large organizations, often international in scope, like Schlesinger Associates, Fieldwork, or Plaza Research, or have banded together as regional groups, or loose cooperatives. I've run many multi-city (even international) studies entirely in facilities belonging to a single organization, which, by the way, can get you notable discounts on their services.

Basically, once arrangements have been made, all you need to do as moderator is to show up. Everything else it taken care of for you; it's a real pleasure. While commercial facilities can be found in most larger cities and their suburbs, they are not truly ubiquitous. For example, while there are, at the time of writing, good focus group facilities throughout the Miami, Florida area as well as in other major Florida cities like Orlando and Tampa, there are none in or close to Palm Beach, which is a major location for research with upscale respondents. There are whole states, like Montana, with very few dedicated facilities. In such cases, you have to find an alternative venue if you need to do in-person research in that location.

One practical downside to in-person central location groups is that participants and moderators have to travel to the facility, along with clients and observers. Within any local area you have to take into consideration travel time and distance, the vagaries of traffic, parking, weather, availability during research hours, end-of-day fatigue, willingness to come to the specific location (e.g., if it's close to participant's homes or work, whether it's in a "good" or dicey neighborhood).

A second downside is that professional facilities are businesses, which means you need to have significant budget available for their services. Commercial focus groups facilities typically charge $500 or more to host a single group (including the room itself), to which you have to add the cost of food, often videotaping, making up copies of guides and other materials, any special equipment required, parking (if in a city), recruiting, administrative and other services (e.g., videostreaming, which can run close to $2,000 a day). Many facilities also charge an additional project management fee.

In-Person at alternative venues

In commercial practice, the most common alternative to using a dedicated facility is to conduct depth sessions in the meeting rooms of a centrally located hotel. I've occasionally conducted interviews in my hotel suite, recruits' offices, homes, workplaces, or interview suites in my research firm's own offices. The bottom line is that you can do depth interviews virtually anywhere that's private and quiet where you can sit down with and interview the person. In this day and age however, you also need to consider security and #MeToo concerns.

Focus groups obviously require a larger space than IDIs, somewhere that all the participants and observers can be brought together, a conference room or other large, private space that can be set up with a table around which to seat group members and, ideally, a separate space in which to seat clients or other observers, if any will be present.

Most often, commercial focus groups outside of central location facilities are done in hotel conference rooms. Typically when doing depth research in hotel settings you secure two rooms, one serving as focus group or interview room and the other as "back room" from which the research team can monitor the group. For focus groups, the front room has seating for participants and a moderator around a large table (often one or more folding tables bunched together). A smaller room and table would work for interviews. A video camera is normally set up in the front room that transmits what is going on to observers in the second room, today possibly over WiFi or via in-wall Ethernet.

The same organizations that run facilities can typically set up and manage such alternatives for you, providing the same basic services as they would in their own offices. This is not a particularly cost-effective alternative to central location groups. In fact, it often runs appreciably more to rent conference rooms and contract for those services than it would to use a central facility.

This type of setting is rarely as comfortable and smooth-running as the professional facility. While conference-room groups usually work out pretty well, glitches can occur. I will never forget the time I attended a focus group session at an historic Hilton hotel in London. My role was largely that of an observer since an English partner company was responsible for doing the U.K. and European research. Well, the video link broke down a few minutes after the moderator began the group so my colleagues and I ended up in the old servant's passageway behind the conference room, cracking open the door at the rear, crouching there and observing the groups as best we could through a six-inch opening. It was comical, like something out of a Marx Brothers movie. And it also illustrated one of the key demands on the professional moderator that I cannot emphasize too often — coping with Murphy's Law. You must be unflappable, willing and able to adapt to whatever comes up!

Sometimes the two-room set-up is not appropriate. For example, as related in the Introduction, my very first focus group was held in a single hotel conference room with the client sitting at the table and a recorder on the table. The topic was extremely sensitive and we felt that these men would not be comfortable or willing to speak candidly if there were unknown, faceless observers watching and recording from a different room.

In applied social science and employee research, given cost and logistic considerations, it may be appropriate to conduct focus groups in conference rooms provided by the client or in a public space like a community center, library or, perhaps, city or agency offices. In such cases, you may or may not have someone serving as host and you may have to take responsibility for logistics such as greeting and signing in participants, recording the session, and handing them their honoraria.

Recently I was part of a team assigned to do employee focus groups for an insurance company that had just merged with a competitor. The primary research objective of this project was to understand how the employees of the two companies perceived their organizational culture and how that related to their own personal values, as well as how they perceived the culture of the other firm, with the goal of helping management merge the two cultures to create a win-win for all. It was a large, rush project: four of us were each assigned several offices around the country, to conduct three focus groups in one week's time. The client did arrange a coordinator to assist us in these locations and assigned 12 employees to each group, eliminating the need for us to recruit them.

The groups were held in office conference rooms, around a rectangular table. We were provided with Sony digital recorders and remote 360° microphones to place at the far end of the table (we used an Olympus "boundary" microphone that looks like a little flying saucer), recruitment lists, and tent cards with an employee's first name on it in separate stacks for every group. Each office was asked to make up enough copies of the stimulus materials for our groups. The offices had been asked to have a whiteboard or a flip chart in the room, as well. At the end of the day, we'd travel to our next city, check in to a hotel, go online and send in our MP3 recordings of the day for transcription, get up the next morning and do the next round of groups.

This worked pretty well, although attendance was rather uneven and, in some offices, the chairs we were given to use were oversized so that tables became very crowded. In a few cases, there had been a mix-up in the name cards so that, say, my 9 AM group turned out to be the people listed in the attendance sheet for 11 AM, or individuals turned up in a different group than the one to which they were supposedly assigned, had no name card, said their name was misspelled, etc. One of my offices had a white board (unfortunately, not the kind that prints out what is written on it), and one had a flip chart, but the other two had neither, so I had to tape sheets of paper to the wall in order to record values as group members called them out. I made it all work out, but that took some doing. Again, a moderator needs to be unflappable and willing to improvise as needed.

Telephone depth interviews and focus groups

There is a dramatic difference, in my experience, between these two modality options.

Telephone depth interviews

Time-tested, simple and effective, telephone depth interviews ("TDIs") arguably have been the single most popular depth methodology in recent decades, at least in my marketing research practice. Basically, you arrange to call the interviewee at a certain time and then conduct a focused two-way interview over the phone. TDIs tend to range in length from 30 minutes to an hour; much longer than that, it is difficult to maintain engagement, while it is hard to obtain any real depth in less time than that. You'll want to record both sides of the conversation and may need to allow the client team to listen in to at least some of the interviews. In some cases, you may also want to present visual or multimedia stimuli, or physical prototypes. We will discuss some of the ways in which you can set these up at the end of the next chapter.

Telephone focus groups

"Tele-groups" are another time-tested alternative, but one I would generally discourage. They have largely been replaced by online groups but "Tele-groups" may still be worth considering when target participants are geographically spread out or when the time and proximity required to attend in-person groups would be problematic (e.g., for sales reps) and there is no need to show any stimuli, or when computers and high-speed connections are not available or appropriate. Weather, traffic, and other conditions are not likely to affect telephone groups. You can easily schedule them at times convenient for your subjects. Although it can be difficult to keep track of who is speaking and to obtain the same level of participant engagement as with in-person or online sessions, an experienced moderator can get a lot of depth and information from telephone groups. And they are pretty cheap to organize and run.

You need to design tele-groups somewhat differently than in-person groups. Experience suggests that this medium works best for four to, at the very most, six person groups; larger groups than that get confusing and hard to manage. Telephone groups are also less tolerant with regard to length. Sixty minutes tends to be the maximum time you can keep most telephone groups cohesive and involved. It is also more difficult to manage these groups; for example, to prevent participants from talking over one another or to keep them focused on the discussion.

Yet another disadvantage relevant to both depth interviews and focus groups is that interacting over the phone simply does not give the moderator or fellow group members the same density of interpersonal cues as in-person depth interviews or groups. For example, one cannot observe body language, and you may lose other subtle cues. Merely being in the felt-and-seen presence of others facilitates bonding and spontaneous interactions. It tends to be difficult to keep telephone groups focused, interacting, and moving forward, far more so than TDIs where you can build rapport and maintain a more intense connection with the interviewee. Personally, while I have no issues doing TDIs, I am not enamored of telephone groups and would be happy never to do them again, but others may be of a different mind in this respect.

Online focus groups and depth interviews

Everyone, it seems, is talking about online focus groups these days. There is a definite sense, right or wrong, that, like "mobile" surveys conducted via smartphones, this may be the wave of the future. They end up costing at least modestly less than in-person central location groups, since you eliminate the cost of food and travel (which can be significant). Online groups also eliminate the hassle of getting yourself, your clients, and most important of all, your participants to a central location at a specific time, which can be significant as most groups of working people are conducted during the early evening time of heavy traffic.

An even greater (but largely unsung) benefit in my view is that they eliminate the whole issue of geographic location. Online groups can be comprised of individuals tightly screened and selected for specific characteristics but who can participate from any location, home or elsewhere, where they have access to a high-speed internet connection, laptop or desktop computer (or tablet, although smartphone screens remain too small for use in most online groups) and, at least in some cases, a phone line. I have personally done online focus groups from my Portland, Oregon home office with participants across the U.S., from the East Coast to Hawaii, and internationally with individuals located in Europe, the Middle East, East Asia, in which case, it is generally advisable to break them into separate groups by time zone to avoid having some participate in the middle of their night or other inconvenient times.

When I wrote the first version of this book, virtually all "online focus groups" relied on keyboarded questions and responses. The moderator keyboards questions and probes, group members type in their responses, which then appear on everyone's screens preceded by the writer's name. Today, a text-based focus group equivalent might be run on smartphones, perhaps using what we are now calling "texting" (SMS) as a medium of communication.

In the first version of this book I panned online groups because early platforms relied on keyboarded chat, arguing that the tried-and-true methodology of in-person groups was greatly preferable. Shortly afterwards, I started working with the Blackstone Group, Inc. and discovered they had pioneered precisely this with a platform that uses webcams to create a sense of virtual reality for the group, allows lag-free discussion, and also takes advantage of other digital tools.

I started doing online groups using Blackstone Group's proprietary (IQ)^2 technology (short for Innovative Insight from Qualitative/Quantitative) and I have come around to rely on webcam-enabled online focus groups as my default format. Today there are not only a number of in-house platforms for online groups used by research organizations, but you can "rent" the technology by the group from such sources as FocusVision, iTracks, 20:20, and Schlesinger Associates. Apologies to readers of the first version of this book — I eat my hat!

When you manage these groups synchronously and moderate them conscientiously, online groups can offer similar dynamics as in-person groups. A major, and enormously valuable difference, is that geographic location is no longer a meaningful factor when assembling your groups. Additionally, the platform I am most familiar with allows participants to keyboard as well as engage in oral discussion, making active participation easier for individuals who are shy or find it difficult to speak in public. It also offers a virtual backroom for clients and other project team members, from which they can observe the session and communicate with the moderator and one another through keyboarding.

More recently, I have started to use this same platform for depth interviews I would previously have done as "straight" TDIs. An online depth interview (I have taken to referring to these as ODIs) has several potential benefits. First, it is easy to set up once you are familiar with the technological platform and how to manage it. You can have the interviewee just call in or have the system call out to them and link them into the call. Clients and other team members can do the same and, after their own phones are muted, easily monitor the interview. It's easy to record the session, typically with just a click of your mouse. With the platform I customarily use, you have the additional, truly major advantage of that virtual backroom. Additionally, as I will discuss, you can use webcams to create a similar virtual reality experience as when doing webcam-enhanced online focus groups.

Choosing the format

Here are some criteria for choosing between online, telephone and in-person formats:

How to Chose Among Depth Research Formats

Modality	Advantages	Disadvantages	When to Use
In-Person	Familiar/ tried-and-true	Each in a single location	Clients strongly prefer
	Face-to-Face comfort	Highest cost option	Participants fitting selection criteria available in location(s)
	Maximizes interaction	Need enough target sample	Physical objects involved (e.g., prototypes), sensory issues
	Maximizes group dynamics	Travel costs & hassle	Target participants may not be digitally savvy or online
Online	Novel/Digital	Unfamiliar/Digital	Cross-geography groups appropriate/desirable
	No geographic restrictions	No physical proximity	Clients willing to take perceived risk of novel modality
	Eliminates travel, meals, etc.	Must have high-speed internet	Participants comfortable with digital tech & interaction
	Multimodal communication	Everything is virtual	Physical presence unneeded/nothing to handle, smell, taste
Telephone	Convenience maximized	Groups must be small	Small groups acceptable
	Lowest cost/ Minimal setup	Must keep it relatively brief	No visual, physical materials or content involved
	Everyone has phone access	Hard to facilitate group dynamics	Engagement or depth not a primary consideration
	Eliminates travel, meals, etc.	No visual cues, interaction	Cross-geography groups appropriate/desirable

CHAPTER 7

Practical Research Design: Who, How Many, Where?

What will you actually do within any of these options for setting up and conducting depth research? Let's get practical and consider how to develop the optimal depth research design to meet the specific objectives of any particular study.

A simple way to design sample and choose locations for depth interviews and focus groups is by working out your strategy with respect to the following five considerations:

■ 5 Key Design Considerations

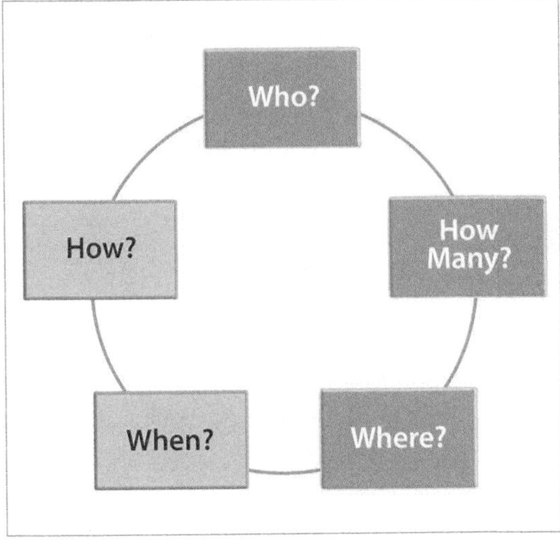

As the graphic suggests there are five interlinked decisions you will need to make. Two relate directly to selecting your sample: Who? and How Many? Two others decision relate more to logistics, Where? and When? We'll start with the three considerations shown in dark gray: Who? How Many? and Where?

Who?

This is the single most important decision you need to make as you begin a depth research design. Review what you seek to find out from the depth research and proceed by working out sample composition; that is, which types of people do you need to talk with to accomplish your objectives?

Define your segments

Think in terms of segments, identifying a reasonable number of discrete, relatively homogenous segments (classes, groupings or types of participants) for which you can spec out concrete, preferably objective recruiting/participation criteria to ensure that you recruit the right individuals. This is analogous to identifying the "cells" to be sampled in a quantitative study. Sometimes you have to do a bit of research to determine just who the right targets are, but that is true of all marketing research and other applied research, qualitative or quantitative.

Although we will not go into detail about recruiting for depth research, there are a few issues one must keep in mind when designing the sample for qualitative studies.

Prevalence

Many of the types of people you seek to research will be relatively high in prevalence and easy to find virtually anywhere, like consumers who shop online, primary care physicians, or people with type 2 diabetes. Others will be of lower overall prevalence but still fairly easy to find in large metropolitan areas. But what if you need to speak with some of the country's few, elite thought leaders regarding HIV disease and its treatment, or pre-surgical transgender individuals over the age of 45 who identify as male? The finer your specifications, the less prevalent your targets will be and the more difficult to recruit.

Unless you are working from lists of prequalified individuals, customer lists, etc., you need to consider how many individuals fitting your desired specifications are likely to be available in the places where you need to draw them from. If you are very lucky, your target audiences will be easy to find and recruit where you need to find them, but don't count on it. Sometimes prevalence is a killer, essentially making your preferred research plan unworkable, in which case you need to adjust your plan, if not abandon it. At other times you can probably pull it off, but you may need to offer significant incentives to get participation and plan on high recruiting time and cost, or go with an alternative to central-location research in commercial facilities, which tend to be found mainly in larger metropolitan areas.

Beware of "professional respondents"

This is principally an issue in marketing research, but it can also extend to legal studies (mock juries) and other types of paid depth research. Beware of "professional respondents," people who, we in the industry suspect, strategically sign up do marketing research and similar types of studies, to boost their income or possibly as their "side gig." Some physicians, for example, do a lot of focus groups and interviews seemingly as a way of supplementing their incomes, while others will not do any marketing research at all, thus limiting the pool of potential research participants. There are also consumers who do a lot of paid research, some to the point of actively seeking out opportunities to participate in focus groups or depth interviews and, potentially, telling the recruiters whatever they think will get them accepted to do the research.

Compounding these issues, many recruiters (and facilities offering recruitment services) develop a list of "friendlies," people who have signed up to do depth research with them or who they have found to be both good research subjects and who are willing to do qualitative research. They often profile these individuals so that they can easily meet researchers' recruiting criteria and, by reducing time and staffing, can give you a better price for their services. They also cull out poor research participants.

While using friendlies is helpful in many respects, it can result in recruiting the same individuals again and again. One healthcare client, for example, asked not to use a certain New York City facility because they supposedly over-use their friendlies. So, for a study with oncologists, I found an alternative venue in Midtown Manhattan, but at least half the group that showed up turned out to be some of the same specialists I had seen just a few months before in the other facility. You might think New York City is large enough to avoid this, but there are just so many oncologists who will do marketing research.

The usual solution to the problem of "professional" study participants is to limit how recently or how frequently individuals have participated in depth research. Very commonly we set an exclusion criterion, such as not having done focus groups or interviews in the past three months or possibly longer.

This does not always work. For example, there was an internist in Chicago whom I'll call Bill. I got to know him pretty well over the years, seeing him regularly when I did physician focus groups downtown. Like other doctors who pad their income by doing depth research, particularly at facilities where participants are paid in cash, he apparently figured out how to game the system. For example, such professional respondents may wait about three months after their last research event, then "batch" invitations, signing up for multiple forthcoming sessions by different moderators at the same time. This way, they can honestly tell recruiters that they have not done research in the past three months or whatever. Anyhow, about two weeks after I saw him in a focus group, I was back at the same facility and there he was, in line for someone else's event. I was early, so we chatted about baseball, which I knew was his passion.

Finding "new blood"

Complicating matters, some prospective recruits tend to be over-researched. These tend to fall into either of two categories.

High-demand, low prevalence

Some types of individuals are over-recruited because they are both highly in demand by researchers and of relatively low prevalence. Oncologists (cancer physicians) are one such group, in my experience, as are small-to-medium business decision makers. Another is the small-to-medium businessperson (SMB) willing to do depth research, particularly those on client's lists, such as utility company's lists of commercial accounts.

Popular locations

Some cities tend to be very popular venues for research due to accessibility, large size, good central location facilities, and also because researchers like going there. These include "A-list" cities like New York, Dallas, Chicago, and Los Angeles. Smaller ones like San Francisco and its Bay Area may also become over-researched for specific topics or segments, in this case HIV/AIDS sufferers and treaters or high-tech engineers, designers, or company employees.

Solutions to avoid the over-recruited

One solution is to seek out individuals who do not participate in a lot of depth research, ideally ones who have not previously done any at all. Facilities and recruiters try to bring in "new blood," sometimes soliciting for people who would like to do focus groups or interviews on Google or even by cold-calling, or have a section of their website asking people to sign up. However, as my oncologist example suggests, even in large markets, it may be difficult to find such individuals, at least for certain target segments. Only a minority of people and, it seems, even fewer professionals and businesspeople will do interviews or focus groups.

Another solution is to go to what are known as "B" or "C" cities that are less often used, at least for marketing research such as Charlotte, North Carolina or Tampa, Florida as opposed to New York City, Chicago, or Miami. Two problems with that are (1) the issue of prevalence; there may not be enough individuals of the segments you need in these smaller places, and (2) you may not be able to find good quality central location facilities in smaller (e.g., "C") cities. For a recent proposal, for example, I could only find a couple of commercial facilities in the entire state of Montana and had to consider alternative venues to obtain reasonable geographic representation. Right now, my favored solution is to do as much research as I can online or by telephone, since that allows you to screen as tightly as you need while drawing participants from virtually anywhere recruiters can find them.

How many?

Once you have defined Who? you can move on to the next key question, How Many? That is how many participants and, as appropriate, how many focus groups do you need or want?

A key difference from quantitative research is that depth methods are not inherently "numbers" dependent. They don't rely on statistics or statistical reasoning. Nonetheless, there is ongoing academic concern about achieving "data saturation" in qualitative research (e.g., Mason, 2010) and, as practitioners, we are sometimes asked about this. For example, just recently, one public agency's request for a proposal to do qualitative research on energy efficiency programs asked specifically about how we would ensure data saturation and I had to explain why that is the wrong question. Just adding sample and employing statistics does not necessarily make your findings more valid or actionable.

Depth methods are what we might call "informant dependent." Who you recruit for interviews or focus groups and then, if doing focus groups, who you put together into any single group are critical questions. Not so much how many.

Clients and even less qualitatively experienced research professionals are often unclear about the point that the statistical principles of sample design central to quantitative research are only incidental to qualitative research. Just adding "more" does not necessarily increase qualitative validity; there is no scientific threshold for how many is enough when doing qualitative research. In fact, "too many" can be dangerous in this context, at a minimum creating an illusion of quantitative certainty. Qualitative work runs on relatively small numbers of respondents.

Exceeding a prudent and defensible number of events and respondents threatens to cross the border from legitimate research into "marketing under the guise of marketing research." In extreme cases this practice has had legal repercussions. I know of at least one situation where the FDA imposed a multi-million-dollar fine on a pharmaceutical company that conducted several dozen focus groups getting physician response to a new drug on the basis that there was no scientific or reasonable basis for doing so many events except to expose the new product and its claims to a very large number of potential prescribers. While that was very lucrative for the research provider, researchers everywhere should always advise clients to "use the tools, don't abuse the tools."

Going back to our question of "How Many?" there are actually five major decisions to be made, one of which applies mainly to depth and interviews, while two pertain only to groups.

How Many?

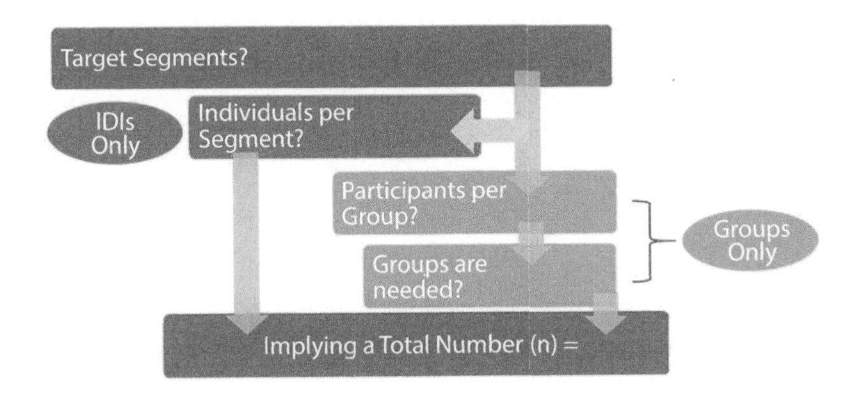

Number of target segments

If you have completed the first step, you have determined the target segments you wish to cover. So you know how many segments you need to consider.

How many individuals per segment for depth interviews?

Working out sample size for depth interviews is generally straightforward. Following the grounded theory principle of continuing to research until you aren't learning anything new (Glaser and Strauss, 1967), my colleagues and I find that 8 to 12 interviewees per segment is a good rule of thumb. Beyond that number, you will generally find that you don't learn enough new information of value from the incremental interviewees.

You can get away with fewer if needed (e.g., due to budget, time, or participant availability) at the risk of not covering all major themes and variations. And there is no actual penalty to doing more except with respect to efficiency, time, and resources. Academic studies tend to go larger, particularly if you can deploy multiple interviewers.

What is the right number of participants for a focus group?

Let's start off by considering how large a focus group should be. There is no simple, cut-and-dried answer. You could theoretically assemble an auditorium full of people and consider that a "focus group" or do the same with an online platform but, realistically, you would be hard pressed to moderate it.

Years ago, I attended a test screening for *Someone to Watch Over Me* at a theater in Hollywood, with dozens of seats and a standard, full-sized movie screen. Each seat had a dial on one armrest that you could turn to indicate your current level of interest as the film unspooled. They'd show an old Mr. Magoo cartoon to calibrate responses and then show the feature they were audience testing. However, while some people might consider that a focus group, it does not fit our definition as it was not moderated. There are, by the way, excellent digital systems for taking such measurements today, either hand-held devices or online programs, which might well be used within the context of a true focus group.

In marketing research practice, a typical "full" group is comprised of from five or six to as many as a dozen individuals. Many moderators find that six to eight group members are generally optimal, whether in-person or online, allowing them to control the group, facilitate positive group dynamics, and get through the entire topical guide. As the group gets larger, these tasks become more difficult, but by no means impossible. More than twelve participants seems to impede group formation, is difficult to manage, tends to result in serial interviewing, and should generally be avoided.

Mini-groups of three to five respondents are another viable option. These are particularly appropriate where you need to interview many different segments, desire more intensive interaction (or more time with each respondent), or where it is not feasible to recruit full groups of each participant type. Particularly at the lower end of this size spectrum (triads), mini-groups allow for the positive aspects of group process while maximizing individual contribution and depth. They also reduce the possibility of "group think," and make it easier to get the benefits of focus groups with hard-to-recruit or low-prevalence subjects.

Dyads are, by definition, the smallest number of individuals that can be considered a "group." Dyads can be managed either more like a group or in almost the same way as an individual interview. In its least sophisticated form, a dyad can serve as a way to compress interviewing time or if a second recruit shows up at the same time when another has been scheduled. Dyads, and for that matter triadic mini-groups, are particularly useful when bringing together individuals with different roles and statuses in organizations or other social systems, to explore their dynamic relationships. Examples are (using triad examples), a mother, father, and child, or an executive, manager, and line worker. Unlike two-person dyads, the odd number of subjects helps to break ties, prevent "face-offs," and keep things moving.

How many focus groups are needed?

Bottom line: one group is never enough for a study, nor is it optimal to conduct only a single group per segment. It is virtually axiomatic that you should not base important decisions on the responses of a few individuals who were willing to attend a focus group in a specified time and place. Sometimes there is neither time nor budget to organize a more robust research program. Still, unless the goal is very exploratory and important decisions do not ride on the results, you should consider other research options before going with an approach that relies on a single group.

Once you specify your segments, group size, research mode, and other parameters, you are ready to tackle the question of how many groups are needed or possible. Sometimes, this is set in stone, for example, when number of groups is specified in the request for proposal and the client is resistant to any changes, often due to budget limitations. Even then, it might be appropriate to try to recommend an alternative research design to the extent that it fits within the available time-and-resources budget.

Most focus group designs use, at minimum, two groups per segment, ideally three or even more if it's a high-stakes or very complicated project, to hedge the odds against a chance result. The importance of multiple groups only increases if the sample is in any way heterogeneous. With a single group, you are pulling together at most just one or two individuals from each sub-type. Even a two-group per segment design should receive a careful evaluation in this respect.

Not infrequently, for practical purposes like time and budgetary limitations, you will need to combine one or more compatible segments to create "collapsed segment" groups. Doing so only increases the importance of conducting multiple groups of each composition.

Calculating the optimal number of groups

Your research strategy (the "how?") will help to shape decisions regarding number of events. For example, if you decide to use triads versus full groups, a larger number might be both feasible and appropriate. If you want to employ an iterative approach, you might want to conduct a certain number of "rounds," which, multiplied by the number of segments you need to hold groups with, can lead to a larger number of events. Nevertheless, for a quick, replicated or evolving design, as little as two groups per segment may be appropriate, and, as noted, even a single group per segment would be the fewest you can get away with.

Unlike depth interviewing, doing focus groups adds the additional consideration of group composition. Regardless of whether you're planning "full" groups of about 8 or mini-groups of 4-5, smaller groups (e.g., triads) or larger ones (if you must), a good starting point is to consider who can, or should, be put together into a group. The general rule is homogeneity to build your groups from individuals who share characteristics relevant to the research objectives and who share enough other commonalities to form a functional group. They have to be enough alike to work together and to represent a functional customer (or other) segment.

Here is a useful way to calculate the optimal number of groups for any single project in four steps:

Determining Number of Focus Groups

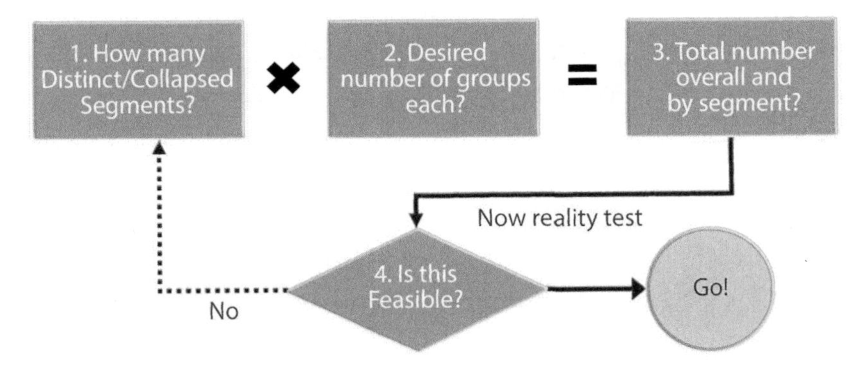

1. Determine the number of distinct (or collapsed) segments you need or want to cover — how many different groupings do you wish to target?
2. Decide how many groups of each type you need or want — that is, number per segment. As we have discussed already, you generally want at least two or three groups per discrete or collapsed segment. For some studies more — sometimes many more in the case of highly heterogeneous consumer segments — would be optimal and sometimes a single group per segment is the most reasonable choice.
3. Multiply these two numbers to get your target overall and by-segment numbers. Again, you would normally multiply the number of segments by two or three to get your desired number of groups (at least in commercial or other settings where time and budget are design constraints).
4. Now, do a reality test. Time and resources (both financial and otherwise, such as moderator, staff, and project team availability, prototypes or other materials) are invariably limited. Also consider prevalence of your targets, in the locations where you might potentially do in-person groups or in the total draw area (country, region, etc.) if you are using online or telephone methodology. Even if you are working from lists (customer lists, voter lists, association membership lists, or purchased commercial lists) remember to consider prevalence when evaluating feasibility.

Don't forget the cost of recruiting your sample and the incentives, if any, you may have to pay for group members' participation. If the number of groups you've come up with is realistic and do-able (and your clients/sponsors are willing to go along), then it's a go. If not, we're back to "you can't always get what you want" in which case, re-evaluate your assumptions and work out an alternative design that at least gets you what you (and your clients) need.

Consider also the time required to implement your design. At least in marketing research, it's the norm to conduct two or even three groups a day and about two weeks to recruit them. If time is the issue, one can use additional moderators to conduct simultaneous groups (assuming you can recruit enough respondents and have the budget for doing it this way). At the very least, you might consider conducting several minigroups representing different respondent types, thus conserving resources.

Single-group-per-segment designs

Optimal is not, however, the same as either necessary or possible. You may sometimes need to employ a single-group-per-segment design if you are conducting multiple groups with a variety of segments. It is better to do at least two groups per segment for the reasons that I recommend against single-group designs, but you can generally get away with it. And sometimes you have to limit yourself to one group of each type, again typically due to time and budget issues, sometimes prevalence. In fact, given marketing research clients who are increasingly cost-conscious, I find myself doing some two-group, two-segment designs with acceptable results.

One valid reason to conduct a single cross-segment group as part of a larger study is when you are conducting groups in more than one language. For example, I just submitted a proposal that includes a single Spanish-language group comprising all segments in addition to a number of single-segment English-language groups. Not only did the client request that design, but the cost of multiple in-language groups with Spanish-speaking moderators simultaneous translation would become prohibitive. Complementing the

Spanish-language group, you would typically conduct a single, mixed-segment English-language focus group in that facility on the same evening to cover that geography.

Alternatives to one-group designs

As a matter of principle, when a client asks specifically for only a single group, it is the ethical researcher's duty to probe the reasons why. The right thing to do, "politics" aside, is suggest alternatives that do not have the potential to mislead observers, create spurious results, or generally fail to meet the client's business objectives, which is likely to be the case, if a decision is hanging on a single six to eight or even ten person group. Sometimes this means recommending a different methodology entirely.

The simplest and, often, easiest with respect to obtaining client buy-in is to consider two mini-groups adding to the same number of participants as the single group would involve. As long as the time is available to implement them, two minigroups vs. a single larger group can avoid problems related to happenstance recruitment of a "bad" group of individuals or results biased by group dynamics due, for example, to a dominant and opinionated group member. This can be a persuasive argument for such a design.

However what do you do when there are target individuals or segments that are too numerous, scarce, geographically dispersed (for in-person) or costly to fit into a reasonable number of focus groups, or even into a single homogenous group? One workaround is to plan some individual interviews to complement or supplement your groups. These can even be with senior-level stakeholders in your clients' organization (for example, at the C-level) to help you plan your groups before you actually go on to design the discussion guide and finalize other plans. Supplementary depth interviews can also cover specific individuals or types of individuals from whom you want to gather intelligence but who would not fit into groups. These can be experts, key opinion leaders, even knowledgeable consultants. For community or public policy studies, for example, you may want to plan a few individual interviews with officials, administrators, organizers, or other leadership.

And the total number of study participants is . . .

In order to complete the design you are developing, you obviously need to find and recruit the target number of participants. By this point, that number should be easy to calculate.

Total number of depth interviews

For individual depth interviews, multiply the number of segments by your desired number of interviewees per segment. For dyads, obviously, you will need two recruits per interview. As suggested for determining the number of focus groups, be sure to reality check yourself. Is this number feasible?

Realistically, don't plan on completing more than ten depth interviews per day and generally eight or fewer. Although some clients like or even demand more, as many as 12 per day, that may not be practicable. Even if enough target individuals are theoretically available, one problem is getting participants to "show" during off-times. With working people you will generally be able to schedule interviews after work, perhaps around breakfast and lunch. You will need to take into account this issue of availability when designing the research and reality checking feasibility.

Additionally, consider your own needs and those of any other interviewers you bring into the project. How many depth interviews of the desired length and intensity can you really do, and do well, within any one day? An exhausted moderator tends to make mistakes, miss things, or "just go through the motions." So consider your own tolerance. I've done up to about 12 interviews a day, but generally find myself less effective after about eight.

So ask yourself: can you complete the target number of interviews within the required timeframe? Within the available resources (taking into account all related costs, such as any incentives)? If not, go back and revise your sampling plan.

If you don't know enough to segment your interviewees, you might want to go larger than the recommended 8-12 per segment, perhaps 15 up to 20 or 25. If you have to set a specific number (as in professional practice where you need to craft a fixed proposal and budget), that's a good range. In the ideal world, you could do 12-15 interviews, stop, evaluate if you need to do more and then recruit and conduct a second set, repeating until you're not obtaining significant new learnings. This is rarely feasible in professional (vs. academic) research.

Total number of focus group participants

Once you have determined the number of groups, number of segments, and target group size, it's a simple matter of multiplication to determine the target number of individuals per segment and total number of participants you need. Once again, reality check for feasibility and affordability. But that's not all that you need to take into account . . .

You can only recruit a fraction of any target population

Just as for quantitative survey research, you can define the population from which you wish to draw your sample, but you cannot necessarily count on recruiting (and completing depth research with) more than a fraction of that population.

As a rule of thumb, you need to find and contact as many as 15-20 individuals who fit a desired profile in order to recruit one for a focus group or depth interview. At times you can get away with less, and sometimes you are forced to settle for less than you'd prefer by circumstances such as prevalence or number of records on client or other lists from which you are recruiting.

When you are working with an in-person methodology, this can severely limit feasibility. Even when doing depth research online you must still ensure that you can find enough qualifying individuals who can and will participate on the designated dates and times to meet your needs. Trying to recruit even one full group of, say, left-handed, blue-eyed 18-to-24-year-olds with a baccalaureate degree, who have three or more children, and shop for groceries online, is probably a futile task. Even in a major city like New York or Los Angeles, this is a tall order. Sometimes you can literally bribe them with a high incentive, or use a truly excellent recruiter (who will probably charge appropriately for the dubious pleasure), but you really need to be realistic. This consideration should go into reality testing your "how many" calculations.

You, your team or a professional recruiter can potentially supplement lists and squeeze out more candidates through any number of strategies, from advertising, using phone books (old school, I know) or other published compendiums, social media, Googling, tapping other online resources, networking, asking thought leaders or other referral tactics (e.g., you might incentive recruits or contacts to recommend others). Particularly if you really have no idea how to locate the right individuals, such as narrowly defined decision makers or other targets within an organization, you might consider what is known as "snowball sampling:" finding a person in a position to know others who might meet your criteria (such as a receptionist in a target organization or type of organization) and asking them for suggestions, then asking the same of those you reach.

Recruit vs. "show"

It's important to keep in mind the fact that you can get a person to agree to participate in an interview or focus group but they may not necessarily show up at the appointed time. "Show" rates are always an issue; you really cannot predict how many recruits will show. It can be embarrassing and costly if you set up a group and only a few actually show up. The same with interviews.

We commonly employ two strategies to maximize show rate. One is to over-recruit for any event. In order to feel confident that six to eight recruits will show for a scheduled eight-person group, it is customary to recruit 10-12. For online groups, given the ease of simply not sitting down in front of your computer and going online, I often recruit as many as 16.

The other is to send reminder emails or, better, phone calls (due to immediacy, impact, and the sense of obligation created when a person promises they will attend). SMS messaging might also be employed. Leaving voicemails is iffy in my experience; recruits may not check them. It appears to work best when reminders are done the same day as the scheduled interview or group, or even emails are sent the working day before and a reminder call the day of.

Where?

Depth research is almost invariably linked to one or more specific geographies, which can be anything from world regions or countries to cities, or neighborhoods. That consideration obviously defines the boundaries from within which you will draw your sample. As suggested, this can affect feasibility with respect to Who? and How Many?

But, getting even more practical, for in-person focus groups and depth interviews you'll need to decide where to hold the events. If this is a regional study, you'll need to stay within the appropriate region, while national and global studies require identifying appropriate markets or regions, and dividing the sample and segments among them.

Location, location, location

Except for geographically restricted studies, larger multiple in-person groups or depth interviews with any single audience or segment are generally conducted across multiple locations. Practically, unless you are recruiting a very common respondent type, it may be extremely difficult to find and recruit enough individuals to assemble more than one or two full groups per segment per location. Similarly, you can only rarely do more than two or at most three days of individual interviews — about the same number of participants — in any single location.

Furthermore, differences may exist in local or regional practices, preferences, cultures or subcultures, and various demographics. This is true even of medical practice, where a few schools or opinion leaders may dominate a city or entire region. Unless you are intentionally restricting your study to a specific, narrow geography or a specific organization, you want to control for such differences to the extent possible by spreading the research around. That means getting a good geographic representation, both of various regions and of city sizes, urban and suburban areas, and so forth.

Much of my depth research has been for clients marketing products and services on a nationwide basis. For such projects, depending on budget and the number of planned events, it is common practice at least to schedule events on both U.S. coasts and somewhere in-between, perhaps also tapping cultural variations of the North and the South. For consumer work in particular, you might target each of the six U.S. Census regions and divisions.

You might also want to target locations selectively, based on the product or service under study. Focus on areas where you are likely to find customers or prospects or where competitors have their strengths, to tap specific ethnic groups, or spread the research across demographically distinct areas (e.g., city, suburb, exurban, rural areas).

Even for local or regional studies, it remains advisable to draw from different areas. For example, when doing research in "Chicagoland," a particularly spread-out region, you might plan to use a downtown facility, others in the northern, southern, eastern, and western suburbs. There are at least two reasons for this: first, to tap potential variations in demographics, socioeconomic status, culture or practices, and, second, to make it easier to find and recruit enough subjects to fill your groups.

Similarly, when I work for a state-wide power utility such as Florida Power and Light, it is customary to conduct groups or interviews with customers in several parts of the state. It would be easiest to tap just the largest metropolitan area — in this case, the Miami metro region — but doing so would not let you detect any differences between those customers and those in other markets with different population composition, demographics, and economic situations.

These considerations are true for in-person, online and telephone groups alike. With the latter two you have the option of drawing groups of any segment from across virtually any geographic locations. For in-person groups, logistics become a major design issue.

Consider where targets live or work

You always need to consider transportation issues, where target respondents live or work and how they will get to your research venue. You will not find many executives or physicians in low-income urban areas such as central Detroit or Camden, New Jersey, for example. You would necessarily want to schedule the research in suburban locations where they are likely to live and where they would be comfortable traveling at night. Interview consumers, particularly if older, ill, or less affluent, where there is good access to public transportation. In some cities, respondents simply will not drive beyond a certain distance or to certain areas, no matter how appealing the facility or logical the location. It is very difficult, for example, to get Dallas and Fort Worth, Texas, respondents to go to a facility halfway between the two cities, such as in Grand Prairie.

Unless you have just one or two respondent segments to cover in separate focus groups, you have to figure out how to divide them up among the different locations you are choosing. The usual solution is to spread them around. For example, you might cover segments A and B in City One, segments A and C in City Two, B and C in City Three, and so forth. This minimizes the possibility of inadvertently biasing your results by doing all groups of the same types in the same cities. In contrast, if you are planning depth interviews, you can generally include representatives of all segments in any one location, unless there are prevalence issues or geographic restrictions by segment.

Find and select venues

Another "where" issue is selecting a venue in which to hold in-person research. When I first started doing focus groups and depth interviews, commercial facilities were relatively few and far between; they still may not be easy to find overseas, even in large cities. This is why we did the London group I mentioned earlier in a hotel. Since I did that research, there has been a proliferation of professional facilities designed for this purpose in virtually any metropolitan area in the U.S. and major Canadian, Latin American, European, and Japanese cities.

Today there may be a wide range of facilities in different locations within a metropolitan area, such as shopping malls, downtown or office centers, and other locations, ranging in style from "very casual" to highly professional and sometimes too slick, at least for my taste. On the other end of the spectrum, I came to dislike mall facilities early on. I recall one in the New Orleans area that offered gold costume jewelry as incentive for consumers, which I thought odd. My biggest problem, however, was that I was doing evening groups with physicians, the last of which ended after the mall closed so we were escorted out through a service passage, past garbage bins, to a door at the back of the mall, far from anybody's car. Be sure to check how the facility handles late groups or interviews if you are using such a facility!

Most research supplier firms and individual moderators have their favorite facilities, sometimes arranging discounts from specific facilities or chains. I keep a file of research facilities on my computer for easy reference. If nothing else, you can search for central location facilities online through Googling or through directories like Greenbook.org (http://www.greenbook.org) or Quirks.com. Of course, if you have them, you can use these organizations' hardcopy directories, which is actually my personal preference since it is so easy to thumb through them to find what you're looking for.

CHAPTER 8

Practical Research Design: When? and How?

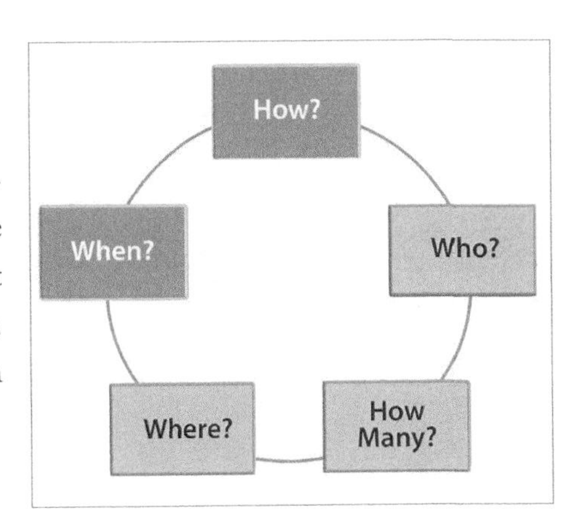

Now, let's explore two final mission-critical considerations. First is the **How?**, which is specifically about planning your research strategy. That leaves **When?**, which is often the last planning decision made.

How?

Before getting into more logistical or execution-specific considerations, it makes sense to think through the key question of how you are going to explore the project objectives with the subjects you have identified. We have already discussed four major formats. Let's consider the major "how" possibilities for focus group research, most of which also apply to depth interviews.

Focus Group "How" Options

DIMENSION	VARIATIONS		
Structure	Scripted	Conversational	Unscripted
Sequencing	Replicative	Evolving	Fully Iterative
Size	Full (6-12 people)	Minigroup (3-5 people)	Dyad (2 people)
Format	In-Person	Telephone	Online
Mode	Fully Qualitative	Some Numbers	True Qual/Quant
Advanced Tactics	Individual Responses	Breakouts	Projective Methods

Structure: scripted versus conversational approach

One key dimension on which focus groups vary is how tightly structured they are. There are three basic variations.

The scripted approach

From textbooks you're likely to get the idea that depth research almost by definition follows a predetermined "script." The research team develops a discussion guide that literally spells out the words the moderator will say, provides a linear structure to the lines of questioning, and gives precise timings for each section of that guide.

This scripted approach treats the focus group guide very much like a quantitative questionnaire where interviewers receive training to ask the questions verbatim. In the most rigorous version of a scripted approach, the mandate is "stick to the script," although most moderators, in my experience, follow the script somewhat more loosely.

A more or less tightly structured approach seems to have become dominant, at least in U.S. practice. Doing so simplifies the moderator's role. It allows her or him to focus more on managing individuals or group dynamics, less on understanding responses and continually flexing the lines of questioning "on the fly" to fit the emergent group dynamics.

A scripted approach is certainly easy on observers (including clients). Everything is very predictable. The moderator follows the script and all the agreed-upon questions are asked and answered. With good probing a competent moderator can still uncover differences between and within segments/types of respondents and get satisfactory insights into the "whys" and "wherefores." In addition, a scripted approach is easier to moderate than the alternatives, placing less demand on the moderator's skill and craft. Little or no substantive knowledge of what is being covered in the session is required; the moderator need not be a subject expert, only a good moderator — rather like an old-fashioned master salesperson who can sell any widget — you hire him to sell based on his skillfulness.

There is essentially no difference between using a scripted approach for focus groups and using that same approach for depth interviews. The discussion guides will be 80 percent or more the same and, except that you will not be facilitating group discussion, the approach is essentially identical.

While this approach is easy to satirize, the scripted option offers good value when used appropriately. For example, it makes sense when you are hiring outside moderators whose aptitude may not be known in advance, or when there is little or no opportunity to work with them to ensure that they fully understand the background and objectives of the research. It is also very handy for research supplier organizations, as this directive and structured method can safely be handed off to junior-level researchers.

The conversational approach

However, the strict scripted approach is neither the original model nor the best way to tap the full potential of depth methods, which in my opinion, is to employ a less structured and more open-ended conversational approach.

The conversational approach begins with developing not a script but a topical guide. This is a relatively brief two- to four-level outline of the topics to be covered in the session, usually with the equivalent of stage directions to remind the moderator to probe specific topics or perform certain tasks. The truly skilled moderator uses the guide literally as a guide. One of the most skilled moderators I have ever worked with, TVG's John McNichol would, in fact, put the topical guide aside and not refer to it again until the end of the session, at which point he would glance over it to make sure everything had been covered. Honestly, I still don't feel comfortable taking it that far.

The moderator sets the agenda by introducing a topic or question, then pretty much lets the interviewee or group conversation take its own path, gently steering and nudging things back on track as appropriate. If a person "jumps ahead" to something later in the topical guide, the moderator's default move is to go with the flow of conversation rather than saying "Pardon me, we'll get to that later," as would be done in the scripted approach.

If discussion veers from the planned path, but reveals new, unanticipated information relevant to the research objectives, the moderator works with that. This is not to say that the moderator should allow a free-for-all. Rather, the skillful moderator employing the conversational approach works with group dynamics to facilitate a discussion that "goes with the flow" of how the participant(s) think and which allows for unanticipated, serendipitous findings.

For example, I was asked to conduct a focus group with multiple sclerosis (MS) patients. The U.K.-based client wanted to determine which of several new self-injection devices to license for a new injectable treatment. The research firm developed "one of those" structured discussion guides, which, as noted above, makes sense when hiring outside moderators. Following up on a seemingly incidental comment by a group member, I uncovered the fact that the prototypes and concepts under consideration by the client, and reflected in the discussion guide, had omitted something very important to MS patients: a "sharps" container for used needles. No one had apparently thought of that, but it has become a big issue in the U.S., since we cannot just toss these into the garbage any more. In fact, several similar issues emerged, none of which were foreseen or provided for in the discussion guide. Just "following the script" might have satisfied the client, but would have led to flawed or at least limited conclusions and recommendations.

Again, the conversational approach and topical guide used for individual depth interviews is virtually identical in format and content to the focus group version. Similarly, you follow the same basic method.

The unscripted approach

Some textbooks and practitioners suggest that the alternative to the scripted approach is a totally unscripted approach. Some form of discussion guide or topical guide is developed, but nothing as detailed or sequenced as with the two other approaches. It may just be a short list of topics or questions.

The moderator introduces a topic, issue, or question and allows the discussion to take its own course. In fact, a focus group moderator might physically leave the room, allowing the group to self-generate its own structure and dynamics, letting group members take the discussion where they will. Before leaving the room the moderator normally introduces some ground rules as part of the introductory section and then watches from behind the one-way mirror, stepping back into the room as needed to move things along or get the discussion back on track.

There are focus group practitioners who frequently employ this approach, at least for some research objectives and respondent types. The unscripted method seems best reserved for general explorations or "feedback sessions." While unscripted groups can yield valuable information as the primary research method, they are more like an open discussion than a focused interview or group depth interview as described in Chapter One. They are not truly focus groups in the classic sense of the term.

Still, a "true" focus group can incorporate some unscripted and essentially moderator-free sections or modules. This may occur spontaneously and inadvertently. For example, a discussion can start before the moderator enters the group room (whether physical or virtual) to kick off the formal discussion. Participant discussions can also ignite when a moderator leaves the room.

Obviously the same unscripted and unstructured approach is not really applicable to depth interviews with the partial exception of dyads. It requires a group to figuratively carry the ball.

Sequencing: replicative, evolving, or iterative

You almost never do a single interview or group and stop. Rather, your design will involve multiple interviews or groups, so you'll need to consider how session two will compare with session one, and so forth. There are three basic approaches.

Replicative approach

The first approach I learned was what I'll term "replicative." You basically follow the same protocol over and over for each group or interview, This model is grounded in a "scientific" approach that views the qualitative data collection process, like quantitative research as, essentially, additive. You do additional events to increase factors like sample size and representativeness. Consequently, you try to keep the basic flow of questioning and other elements of the session constant, just as you would for a quantitative survey. Each session replicates the others, to the extent possible although some differences are inevitable due to probing, any necessary adaptations for different respondent types, and other variables.

A replicative approach seems to be the dominant model for multiple interviews and focus groups today. Like scripted research, it is certainly easy for project team members to follow, easy to analyze, and lends quasi-quantitative authority to findings.

There are two major downsides. One is that you won't learn all that you could since you're using the same lines of questioning each time. The second is that you'll often end up with a recommendation, "more research is needed," which I would generally consider a failure.

Evolving approach

A second approach might be termed "evolving." You let the discussions evolve based on what you are learning or if you can see a better way to go, as long as that helps to address the research objectives. You use what you learn from the first session or two to modify what you do next time around. Those learnings may be positive or they may be negative, but in either case you see potential gain from adjusting or enhancing your approach.

Normally you give the original plan or design a chance unless the first time out was a major disaster. For example, if you're doing two focus groups per evening, you may make minor adjustments but basically stick with the original plan that first day, then, if you and your team are not really satisfied with how things went or you feel you have gotten all that you can (or that all your subjects have to give you) from the original lines of questioning, consider how to optimize the plan for the next set of groups. If you are doing multiple depth interviews in a day, you may want to review how it went and make some adjustments around your halfway point, or finish up the day and then tweak your approach for the next day's sessions.

Usually you'd at least tell your clients and observers that you'll modify the sessions in a particular way, but unless you're making dramatic changes you may want to follow the principle, "it's easier to be forgiven than to get permission." However, some moderators would never risk making noticeable changes without first getting them cleared. Changes from session to session tend to be relatively modest, so that may not be an issue.

At its most basic level, this means continually improving the procedures, flow, lines of questioning, wordings, or stimuli. If participants do not respond well to a particular exercise or line of questioning, modify it until you get what you need and want. If a particular exercise flops the first time around, it makes no sense to repeat the approach to see if it works next time. Not uncommonly, for instance, when we work with positioning or messaging concepts provided by advertising agencies, some (professionals especially) reject out of hand what they perceive to be unsupported, overstated, or improperly worded claims. Rather than keep fighting such resistance, it only makes sense to change the approach or stimulus, by adding "reasons to believe" or rewriting copy to avoid what is being perceived as "Madison Avenue speak."

Another way in which a series of interviews or focus groups can evolve is to take what is learned, move on, and shift to what you do not yet know or understand. Once something is clearly established, why not move on? Alternatively, you may come across unanticipated facts or questions, or new possibilities that you or your clients may want to track down. Why not take advantage of the opportunity to find out what you didn't know to ask about?

This approach has become my norm in recent years, at least when I have the authority or client relationship to get away with it. Generally no problem if it's my project and I'm in charge. However, this may not be the case when one is hired or assigned simply to moderate (and possibly analyze and report) the groups or interviews. As I've already suggested, this approach is particularly well-suited to online methods during which you can keyboard back and forth with clients to make changes on the fly without disrupting the interview or group.

Iterative approach

A third alternative is a more disciplined iterative approach in which you set up a series of "rounds" to progressively refine stimulus materials, messages, or even product concepts based on customer response. While this could certainly be done with depth interviews, I learned this approach with focus groups and have only employed it in that context. The project team uses learnings and feedback from the first focus group (Round One) to evaluate and then modify what is presented to the next group (Round Two), and so on. However, the structure or process of the group is held constant (unlike the evolving approach). In this way, you gets progressively closer to the optimal. It is up to the research team to decide whether to iterate separately segment-by-segment, or round-to-round for all respondents.

Ideally, you continue iterating until there is no further change. Practically, at least in business practice, you need to set a realistic limit on the number of events. While some detractors argue that you cannot predict this in advance, or that iterative methodologies lead to "endless iterations," this approach has proven extremely valuable in many situations and has been, in fact, a key differentiator for some research houses.

Size and format

We have already covered these considerations of group size, interview numbers and the options of in-person, telephone, or online methodology. Basically, select the design that best fits (a) your objectives, (b) the specifics of who you need to speak with and their availability, (c) your budget/resources, and (d) client preferences (back to "where the client is coming from").

Mode – qualitative to quantitative mix

A "pure" focus group in the original tradition is completely qualitative. Although you might get some "counts" for exercises like having group members rank order or vote on preferences or asking for a show of hands, those numbers are not treated as data. While they do provide some insight into trends, the moderator will use these numbers to pick the group's collective brain, as a springboard to get at their underlying thought processes, attitudes, or judgments. Although we might report the count, the centerpiece of the analysis is not "how many?" but "why?"

Quantitatively enhanced approach

There is a middle way between a purely quantitative and a true qualitative/quantitative approach, which I would characterize as qualitatively enhanced. Few of us can afford to be true purists, if only because clients commonly want at least an ordinal sense of respondent preferences, valuations, or priorities. Clients, as we've discussed, generally don't fully appreciate the difference between qualitative and quantitative and want at least some "numbers" to go on. Even though the "whys" are far more important than the "how many," it appears that today's focus groups tend to be at least somewhat quantitatively enhanced. They include at least some rankings, ratings, prioritizations, which researchers incorporate into the results as part of the analysis and potentially use to help guide or at least inform business decisions. In other words, we can, when and as appropriate, show them the numbers.

There is nothing wrong with this, so long as it is clear to the project team (and in any reporting) that these numbers are not statistically reliable, valid, or projectable. For example, one to three focus groups will yield from eight to twenty-odd observations, below any reasonable threshold for statistical reliability or validity. The numbers don't rise to the level of true "data," but merely reflect the opinion of a small, non-random opportunity sample of focus group participants.

Most of my depth research today, focus groups especially, is quantitatively enhanced by design and personal preference. I typically use numeric polls that resemble survey questions and are completed individually by group members before any discussion. This gets each person to "put a stake in the ground." While this can be done in central location groups with printed handouts, so that every participant is asked identical questions in the same way each time, online focus group platforms take what I call "numeric polls" to another level. You can just pop up a single-answer or multiple-choice poll, have group members complete the question(s) individually, then share and discuss results. Responses can be tallied within and across groups and shared with clients, including means, modes, even medians.

True qual/quant

Once you reach about 30 observations (four groups or more), simple univariate statistics and even more advanced analytics can be applied. Still, such "data" drawn from focus groups or interviews should be treated with some caution due to the fact that, more than formal surveys, groups normally cover different target segments and depth research participants represent an "opportunity sample" drawn from that minority of specified types of individuals able and willing to attend a group (or to log into an online focus group platform) at a particular place, day, and time. Again, the role of qualitative research is to provide insight, sensitize users to the realities of what's going on, help us form hypotheses or theories, and answer practical questions, not to provide definitive, statistically valid, and reliable data, counts, and measurements.

There is the option of a true qualitative/quantitative approach (or as my Blackstone Group colleague, Kathi Rose aptly termed it, "chimeric") in which you graft a legitimate quantitative exercise onto the qualitative event, cumulate the responses, and then subject the data to formal statistical analysis. Typically, this takes the form of giving focus group members a survey to complete after the qualitative portion of the session. It can be either pencil-and-paper, having them use computers, or even smartphones, to complete a questionnaire, or sending participants in an online group to another server hosting a true online survey. This can also involve multiple polls conducted during the session.

Creative variations on this include developing a program to "crunch the numbers" for that group on the spot and provide some kind of output, which can then be explored qualitatively with the re-assembled group. Such "bells and whistles," in addition to providing valuable stimulus for discussion and insight into response patterns, can be very appealing to clients and have been employed by savvy researchers at least since the early 1990s.

However, the bottom line remains that data from focus groups should not be quantitatively analyzed and reported until or unless an acceptable sample size is reached and, to the extent possible, formal statistical procedures are followed. Some advanced analytical methodologies like Bayesian analysis can be employed with relatively small sample sizes, so that those with the necessary capabilities can do excellent qual/quant research today in the context of focus groups. However, this does not eliminate statistical issues associated with the nature of focus group samples.

Advanced tactics

Individual moderators and research houses have their own, often proprietary (and trademarked) tweaks and tactics, and there are a number of books that provide additional ideas (e.g., Bystedt, Lynn, and Potts, 2011) but I'd like to call your attention to three general types of advanced focus group tactics.

Individual-level responses

Often you need or want to get individuals' immediate, personal responses to questions, or concepts ahead of the potential influences of other group members. While depth interviews by definition give you individual response, you may want to use the same basic tactics for key questions. That way, you get the interviewee to "put a stake in the ground" before you probe and discuss further, while it can also enable you to simulate survey research by getting everyone to respond to the same set of identically worded questions across your sample, making it easier to compare and contrast responses and even do some statistical analysis.

Self-explicated method

The simplest way to do this in central-location or telephone formats is to have everyone write down a brief response (whether in words or numbers), perhaps on a printed self-evaluation form, and then, to take advantage of group dynamics, have them share what they wrote down with the group, then moderate a discussion. These are sometimes termed "self-explicated" methods.

Online polls and quizzes

When using an online platform such as the one I have shown earlier, my preference is to use the "poll" capability and get either numeric or short answer responses from each group member and then broadcast the results, without names attached, to the group as a whole as a stimulus for directed discussion. Here's an example from an actual online focus group:

Which of the following "voluntary" benefits, if offered by your employer, would you be interested in?

Option	%	n
❍ Dental Insurance	0%	(0)
❍ Vision care Insurance	3.33...	(1)
❍ Accident Insurance	0%	(0)
❍ Critical Illness Insurance	3.33...	(1)
❍ Long-term disability Insurance	0%	(0)
❍ Life Insurance	0%	(0)
❍ Pet Insurance	3.33...	(1)

Each group member automatically sees only what they have entered, but the moderator and observers (to whom you grant appropriate rights) can see the summary as shown. You can then "broadcast" these results to the group members as a stimulus for discussion. For group members, results are anonymous — no names are attached — but there is also a switch that allows you and others in the "back room" to see who gave each response.

The written statements or responses to short-answer polls are valuable inputs to subsequent naturalistic or content analysis. This same general idea can easily be adapted to ratings, rankings, likelihood of use, or other "numbers," which I typically also provide to clients in Excel. Again, treat those numbers as qualitative, not quantitative data unless you have an adequately large sample size.

Gallery method

Another useful individual response method is the "gallery approach," which I learned from UK colleagues years ago. Although it could be adapted for individual interviews and online focus groups, it is principally relevant to in-person groups.

- Place stimulus materials, such as visual and/or text advertising concepts around the room, perhaps mounted on the walls.
- Each focus group participant is given a set of evaluation sheets, perhaps on a clipboard in random order (to avoid order effects), and instructed to go around the room at their own pace and complete the evaluation sheets.
- When everyone is done, the moderator asks group members to share their evaluations and facilitates a group discussion.

Breakouts

A less commonly used tactic is to conduct a full-sized focus group and, at an appropriate juncture, break it into smaller work teams. For this, you would ideally have access to separate rooms for each team, although I have occasionally had group members move their chairs around and form two or three groups either at different parts of the table or in different sections of the front room. It is helpful to assign separate members of your team to facilitate each breakout group where you are not present, although I have managed several breakout groups on my own. These teams might engage in brainstorming, product evaluations, role plays, or other small-group exercises, then share their "findings" with the larger group. These are ideally odd-numbered teams of three or five. This approach is based on the practices of the late Ron Lippitt, who co-founded the National Training Laboratory.

This tactic can also be employed with online groups, assuming your software platform allows, although you will probably be limited to two breakout groups. Ideally bring in a second moderator to work with the second breakout team. Honestly, while I have proposed this variation, I have never yet had a client take me up on it.

Projective techniques

Projective techniques, as you are undoubtedly aware, are a classic way to get at emotional and other non-rational levels of response by asking respondents to use their imagination so as to reveal their thoughts and feelings indirectly. They are most easily employed in the one-on-one interview context. While some projective methods are easily done in the focus group context, others that require more active imagination work or self-disclosure can be tricky to use in the focus group setting, although I have had success using even some of the most "far out" techniques with groups.

It can be very difficult for self-conscious individuals to "play" roles like that in the presence of their peers. This is also a problem for high-status individuals and professionals who feel it necessary to maintain face and appear rational in the presence of others. In general, it is easier to get consumers and children to participate in such activities than lawyers, businesspeople, or physicians. Nevertheless, it is possible to do so, as long as the methods do not potentially embarrass or force participants to act "out of character." You can mitigate the problem of acting out of character by using the individual response option, but it really requires careful selection of projective techniques for use in the focus group setting.

Practicalities

When designing focus groups, you must consider practicalities, as you would for any research project. It is important not only to plan carefully with regard to meeting the research design, but also to prepare for the inevitable "snafus," which are likely to occur. I have run into problems due to hurricanes in the East and fires in the West. Sometimes you can plan around these (e.g., parades or construction detours), but not always.

Even if somebody else is in charge of setting up logistics, a smart moderator does not take his or her hands completely off the approach. For instance, when you hold groups during or around mealtimes, it is important to provide appropriate food to respondents and observers. For the most part, ordered-in food is superior to what the facility makes, if they offer such a service. In the U.S., the project team in the back room often expects a very nice meal, so it is prudent to let them order what they want, such as sushi or Italian, or whatever. Most professional facilities today offer menus from a number of local restaurants for this purpose.

The front room generally gets something less fancy. However, whatever you serve make sure it is appropriate; it can be very embarrassing, for example, to serve cardiologists or weight loss groups meals like pasta with an Alfredo sauce. That happened to me once. Salmon in a heating tray can be unappetizing and stink up the room. That also happened to me. Worse, I once had to deal with a situation where the facility ordered deli sandwiches for a largely Jewish focus group, during Passover!

In addition, you must take into account moderator practicalities. A moderator cannot do a set of evening groups in New York City and be able to do an in-person morning group in the Midwest or Pacific region. I have found it easier to work cities from East to West, as then time is on your side. You need to take such logistics into account, and also the idiosyncrasies of today's travel, such as the availability of flights, travel time to and from facilities on the ground, the probability of various kinds of delays due to weather, security, and the like. As we all have experienced, it is no longer prudent to plan to rush to and through airports and then grab a quick cab, Lyft or Uber to the facility.

You can easily be held up on the ground during thunderstorms (in the summer) and snowstorms (in the winter). I have experienced this when trying to get to focus groups in cities like Chicago, NYC or Atlanta. It is best to plan for such contingencies and to leave enough time to handle these delays as they crop up, which they almost invariably will. It is best to leave extra travel time, even if it is inconvenient or adds a bit of cost. That can mean coming in the day before an event rather than taking a chance that everything will go smoothly. This is different from scheduling (and incurring costs) exclusively for the moderator's ease or convenience.

Still, an exhausted moderator or one who loses the ability to focus strategically on the specific group is less valuable. For most, three groups a day is a stretch, two groups a day is the norm. One can possibly moderate as many as four shorter groups in a day. Ideally, there will be some breaks between them. A typical three-group schedule with working respondents might be a breakfast group and two back-to-back after-work groups.

It is always prudent to be conservative with respect to complex designs, since Murphy's Law applies here, as everywhere in life: "what can go wrong might go wrong." And something undoubtedly will!

Incentives

Paying study participants is one of the practicalities you may have to deal with. At least for marketing research, mock juries, and other commercial depth research, even consumers expect to be paid an honorarium, like doing in-person, telephone and online research with 2019 prices ranging from as low as $25 (although this is rarely enough these days) to $150 or more for less prevalent, hard-to-recruit types, the more affluent or more "entitled." Business and technical people, professionals, and healthcare providers can command as much as $300 to $400 or more. It all depends on the local going rate.

Typically, you can offer a slightly lower incentive for online research and no incentive at all for employee research, focus groups with association members, and some types of applied social research. However, unless participation is essentially mandatory (as in employee research) or regarding something about which group members will be highly motivated and engaged, you can rarely get away without some kind of financial incentive. Although I have sometimes been able to do un-paid depth research with consumers, such as utilities' residential customers or trade-allies, particularly if we can draw on a very large list of potentials (e.g., in the thousands) so that the cost of having to contact many prospects in order to recruit your requisite number is offset by absence of incentives, this rarely works today, but may still be worth trying, for non-commercial, low-budget projects in particular.

How much is enough

So how much do you have to offer as an incentive? This is a classic case of "it depends" on the who, the where, your budget and what can best be termed "market conditions." Recruiters and facilities generally have a good idea of what that might be, as do busy researchers and, if you are lucky enough to have one, field departments. Ultimately, just as for screeners, it is prudent to rely on your staff or the recruiting agency for advice on incentives.

Sometimes, if recruiting is going too slowly or poorly, you may want to try increasing incentives. But, please, don't go hog-wild. As long as 20 years ago, I heard about researchers who were offering ridiculously high incentives, such as $800 for a physician specialist to do focus groups. That only bids up the market and takes resources away from research to what amounts as bribes to participate.

In any case, it is customary to pass through incentives to the client at cost; they are a price of doing business. In recent years, I have had excellent results offering emailed Amazon, Visa/MasterCard or similar gift cards as incentives for online groups but something more immediate is the rule for in-person attendance.

When?

You need to be smart about selecting the times for doing depth research. Once you have figured out how many groups or interviews you need and where you want to hold them — online or in specific venues, you can work on scheduling.

Setting the first day of research

When can you start "field," what can and should be the first research day? This is partly a matter of your (and your project team's) schedule. Commonly, the client pre-ordains the starting and ending field dates in their RFP, or at least they specify when they expect the final deliverables. In any case, you need to structure timing so that you can start as soon as you and the project team are ready (available, along with any materials or concepts, prototypes, etc.) and finish in time to allow analysis and reporting within the agreed-upon timeframe.

Everyone is in a rush these days. Clients not only want it done right and cheaply but they also want it fast, which is often an impossible situation unless they are willing to make some trade-offs.

First of all, it's necessary to realistically estimate the time required from project kickoff to the first event. You will need to establish and get client sign-off on recruiting criteria, develop a screening questionnaire that your recruiters will use to qualify prospects accordingly, often allow time for any sample lists to be provided to recruiters or, in some cases, for recruiters to create their own lists or go through whatever preparatory process they follow, and then allow enough time from start of recruiting to the first interview or group.

Facilities and professional recruiters can usually recruit even a relatively hard-to-recruit group or interviews in about two weeks from the time of authorization to proceed. However, this can vary so it is essential to:

- Work with competent professionals
- Heed their feedback and suggestions
- Lock in your facilities before leaping ahead and committing to a specific schedule

Occasionally I have been able to bring off a shorter time when using client lists or "friendlies," but that can be unnerving. Also figure in the time required for you, your team, or the client to develop any stimulus materials as well as for finalizing your discussion guide. This often can be done while recruiting is in progress.

When doing online or telephone research, the same general principles apply. The principal factor determining when you can start remains how long it will take to recruit. In my experience, this has been a particular problem when working from client lists that are not up-to-date or do not contain necessary contact information or from third party lists that turn out to be of poor quality — full of outdated or incorrect names or contact information, or lots of duplicates. I've also tried to recruit using well-known sample panels that employ the same methods to recruit focus groups as they do for quantitative surveys, which has led to rescheduling "make up" groups or dissatisfied clients. You can waste a lot of time and money if you do not execute on these steps and clients are not typically forgiving about failures.

Venue availability

When doing in-person research, even assuming that everyone who needs to attend signs off on your target dates, your schedule may be constrained by availability of the venues you have selected. In particular, the most desirable facilities in any area are commonly booked well in advance. If you are lucky, the times you need in the places you need are available. Too often, that is not the case. When professional facilities are booked, they realize that projects may not start on time (or at all), so they will often place you on a first, second, or even third "hold." This happens especially often with group rooms during preferred focus group times and days (discussed below). In any case, accepting a hold is always a risk. If they cannot clear those holds for you, you must decide whether to postpone or go elsewhere to meet your schedule. Unfortunately, this happens a lot. If possible, hunt around to find an acceptable venue rather than accept a hold situation.

Day of the week

The best days of the week for most depth research are Tuesday, Wednesday, and Thursday. It is rare to schedule either interviews or groups on weekends, and tends to be very difficult to recruit people to give up free weekend time to participate. In fact, it is inadvisable to schedule events on Friday evenings, as this is a time almost nobody wants to do anything like "work." Scheduling interviews early on Mondays or even Monday evening groups, while sometimes necessary, is somewhat risky because it limits the opportunity to confirm appointments and remind recruits to show. These considerations are true regardless of the research mode, in-person, online, or by telephone.

Session length

So how long is a focus group or depth interview? Once again, it depends.

There is no set norm for individual depth interviews but they normally run from 30 to 60 minutes. However, while clients sometimes think you can compress a depth interview into 15 minutes or an even shorter time, that is really more appropriate for a structured interview. Although you may have to be flexible in this regard when clients demand, a quarter hour or less doesn't really leave enough time for introductions and then questioning in any depth. Thirty minutes is a more realistic length for an especially brief interview although, in my experience, most depth interviews run from 45 to 60 minutes.

It's hard to keep a person focused, engaged, and alert for even 60 minutes, but sometimes sessions will run longer. I have, in very rare cases, conducted 90 minute or two-hour interviews, for example when I was exploring with world-class primary medical researchers where they expected HIV treatment to go over the next ten years. They received a $1,000 honorarium and, in a couple cases, dinner at a fancy restaurant. It all depends on what is needed to get the job done.

Focus groups, whether in-person or online, are typically scheduled within one to two hour time slots. Ninety minute and "two hour" groups have been the most common in my experience, with at least five of those minutes at the start of any group for introductory matters, like explaining the purpose of the group, how to participate, disclosures regarding confidentiality, and participant self-introductions. Occasionally, you can complete the objectives for a group in just 60 minutes. For me, that's a stretch but other moderators (probably using more structured, replicative technique) not infrequently conduct one-hour groups.

I have heard of 30-minue focus groups, but I cannot imagine voluntarily choosing that short a time as you'd only have about 25 minutes for the actual research and that just doesn't seem either to allow enough depth of discussion and probing to meet "serious" project objectives or to offer enough informational value to justify the cost and hassle of doing a group.

Scheduling events within each research day

Focus groups are typically conducted in the evening to allow participation after work — typically two groups per evening, one around 5:00-7:30 PM (in part depending on traffic considerations and work schedules) and another about two hours after that. If you're doing two interviews in an evening, you want to schedule the first as early as feasible. By about 10:00 or

10:30 PM, people often become too fatigued to participate fully and actively. You can sometimes do breakfast and lunchtime groups, depending on the type of participant and when they are likely to be available (and willing), or even late afternoon but pre-dinnertime groups with retired people, homemakers, students, or people who work part-time.

Non-working recruits, such as homemakers, unemployed or retired people can often be scheduled at other times during the day. Primary through secondary school students (and their teachers) can often be scheduled in the afternoon, while college and university students can be scheduled at times during their day when they do not have classes.

Sometimes you can schedule events during a target's workday. Employee groups are often scheduled during the work day.

For international research using online technology or just being done by phone, you need to provide similar timing for the participants, even if that means you do the groups at 3:00 AM. It's your participant's local time that matters, not the moderator or project team's convenience.

Individual interviews can, at least in theory, be scheduled throughout the day and through the evening. As part of the recruiting process, potential interviewees are commonly offered a selection of days and times. However, once again working people tend to be available mainly after work. While many professionals, such as physicians, can at least theoretically schedule interview time during the workday, you most often can get a few around breakfast and lunchtime, but will have long gaps mid-morning and afternoons. Business-to-business research, when you are in a position to interview your targets while on the job, can often be scheduled during the workday (particularly telephone and online interviews). Facilities can often help to ensure that mid-morning and mid-afternoon time slots are filled and the interviewees show, but be prepared for a higher rate of no-shows in these "off" times.

Commonly, recruits for 8:00-10:30 pm time slot groups or interviews come to the session already fatigued and somewhat burned-out by their day's activities. Their conversations are more likely to sputter out; you may find them looking at watches and clocks toward the end of the group, even if they arrived late. It is very common when doing two groups per evening that the earlier group tends to be livelier, but sometimes there is no option, and it becomes the moderator's task to make later groups work.

Think in terms of time slots

Think in terms of *time slots* because there is another consideration you must build into your schedule: whether sessions will be conducted back-to-back or with a planned gap in-between. In the past, I almost always set up groups back-to-back. Most of our work was with physicians and other professionals who participated in the research after their workday, so it was important to avoid running so late that they would become over-fatigued, lose engagement, or even nod off on you (which has actually happened, not a few times). So those two hours, at least for the first group, actually ran about 110 minutes to allow changeover, and a 90 minute group would actually be about 80 minutes long.

Recently, especially when working with consumers, it has become increasingly common to schedule a second group to start on the half hour after ending the first group. This avoids problems if the first group "runs late," pushing off the start time for the second group. This is not generally a problem with 90-minute evening groups. However, it can push a second two-hour group into that "late" zone where respondent fatigue becomes an issue.

Similarly, it is wise to leave time between depth interview time slots as well as to schedule in meal breaks. In addition to the reasons I've just discussed for groups, it is extremely hard for the moderator to maintain concentration and energy doing one interview after another, after another.

Time zone

For national or global studies, in particular, time zone is a relatively minor but still important practical consideration for in-person groups. It is a more significant issue for cross-geographic online (or telephone) groups. It would be very difficult to get recruits from East Asia, Europe, and the U.S. into the same synchronous group. Sometimes you have to schedule online interviews or groups outside the U.S. or require the project team to listen to or watch a session remotely in the middle of the night, just due to time zone differences, although it is best to minimize such inconveniences. Even for central location studies, if project team members wish to observe the events in real time, you need to work out times that fit their needs.

Holidays

Don't forget about holidays. They will mess up your schedule. You need to work around at least major holidays (and likely "away" periods surrounding them) such as Christmas, Thanksgiving, July 4, Easter, and New Year's. Also pay attention to religious holidays, particularly those relevant to your target population. You're not going to get even less observant Jewish recruits on the High Holidays or other major religious holidays like Passover. Similar constraints exist for many Muslims and highly observant Christians. If you do not account for these issues you may, at a minimum, embarrass yourself and your client.

Holiday unavailability is even more of an issue in many countries outside the U.S. as many countries and societies celebrate a lot more "bank" and religious holidays than we do. For that matter, pay attention to national vacation seasons and patterns. For example, although European countries may stagger vacation periods, there are whole months during the summer when it will be extremely difficult to schedule any research with businesses or even consumers.

Delayed starts

I have found that the nominal start time for online groups, in particular, can become an issue. You or your team often need to work with the arriving attendees to get their technology up and running. Webcams are often a problem in this respect. For example, sometimes if people have other programs or windows open on their computers, their webcams won't function properly. They may not actually know how to use their webcams (despite what they told the recruiters during screening) or there may be some kind of glitch on their end. There can also be problems hooking up their audio. It's a prudent rule to allow a half hour or so between the time you ask online group participants to log on and the actual start time, so that a 90-minute interview actually needs a two-hour time slot and a two-hour interview needs a two-and-a half hour time slot.

I have rarely had this kind of issue with individual online interviews, although interviewees may sometimes not log in or be at their computers on time and there may be other glitches, so you may actually lose up to about 15 minutes. So it's best to leave some slack, if only in when you schedule online interviews to start.

Sometimes, you may not be able to start in-person groups or interviews on time. This most often happens in the early after-work time slot due to traffic or other delays such as finding the location or parking. Groups or interviews scheduled during the day may also need to be delayed for similar reasons or just because some people generally tend to "run late." It's a good practice, then, to plan at least slightly longer time slots than the nominal session length.

Telephone interviews have almost never presented such problems although, as for any research event, some recruits won't show, may be hung up on another call, etc. In-person interviews present similar issues as described above, so it is prudent to schedule at least a half hour's time between IDIs. Sometimes you don't have an option to do so, but that's really a best practice.

Pacing yourself

It's very easy to forget that you are only human; you need to pace yourself. Generally, you want to get the project done in the minimum time practical. That means looking at your overall design and developing a reasonable timeline, taking into account the project team's schedules, practicalities of travel, season, and so forth.

In the past, team members' availability to take the time away from work necessary for travel was a major consideration. With the availability of online formats and video streaming (i.e., sending real-time video directly to each team members' computer), it is far easier and less time consuming for observers.

It would be ideal to allow a minimum of a few days between at least the first and subsequent days of research in order to get the project team's feedback, decide on any changes to the discussion guide or stimuli, and produce any revised materials, or make other changes. Most often, however, unless you are doing systematic iterative research, you will not have that but will need to conduct groups as close together as feasible.

When scheduling events during the day or evening, don't forget your own needs, such as meals, bathroom breaks, and just plain fatigue. I'll be talking more about this later, but it's important to leave time for meals when working during the day (you can often catch up on dinner after you're done), leave some open time for "bio breaks," and don't expect to do interview after interview or group after group without some "off time" to recharge, think about what you've learned and how things went, time to walk around, take a stroll, meditate, otherwise relax, or even snooze if you can take naps.

It's a matter of what works for you. Depending on the practicalities of travel (see below), team and moderator tolerance, and whether one or more moderators are employed, subsequent groups may be scheduled on two, three, or even four days a week for as long as needed to complete the research design. For a single moderator, two days a week is most common, three days a week if necessary to meet the timeline. This is the same regardless of format.

Wrap up

This has been a lengthy, intensive discussion of what goes into designing focus groups for maximum impact. Why have we detailed the issues? Because you "get what you pay for," even if the cost is really just putting in time and effort to get it right. Consider the following checklist when planning focus group research. Once you have worked through the list, you will be ready to craft a winning (or at least complete and well-designed) research proposal and to move forward translating your design into discussions guides and other materials and then to actually do the groups, which will be discussed in detail in the rest of this book.

Depth Research Design Checklist

☐ 1. Format	Choose among in-person (professional facility or other), telephone, or online
☐ 2. Who?	Identify your research subjects (targets and segments into which they fit)
☐ 3. How	Plan key design elements
☐ a. Structure?	Scripted, conversational, unscripted (for some elements only)
☐ b. Sequencing	Replicative, tactically evolving, fully iterative
☐ c. Size/ Composition	Segments/targets to be included, size and composition of groups
☐ d. Mode	Fully qualitative, quantitatively enhanced, or true qual/quant
☐ e. Advanced tactics	Decide which, if any, you will employ
☐ 4. How many?	Determine number of group/interviews per segment and, from that, total number
☐ 5. Where?	If in-person, where to hold the sessions (location & venue); if online/telephone, from where to draw participants
☐ 6. When?	Draft timeline including when to start recruiting, days/dates and times for interviews/groups

PART 3

MODERATING AND ANALYZING FOR ACTIONABLE RESULTS

CHAPTER 9

Success Strategies for Moderators

To be a moderator or depth interviewer (which, being essentially the same, I will refer to both as "moderator") is to be at once strategic and pragmatic, directing your actions to accomplish the objectives of the project and to manage both your front-stage audience (the focus group or interviewee) and your backstage audience (team members and other observers). At the same time, you need to be prepared to deal with whatever comes up that you did not plan for, and, undoubtedly, something will.

It's all theater

The first thing to point out is that: It's all theater. Literally, being a moderator is a performance in which you are the director, prompter, and facilitator of an improvisational theatrical event even while you are on stage enacting the part or role of "moderator." You are not only managing the action in the focus group room, but you need to keep aware of and seek to manage your back-stage audience — clients, other team members and observers — and the impressions they take away from your act and from the group. Even more than that, as we'll cover later, you need to be aware that they and your project will be "on stage" from their perspective of their-own internal audiences ranging from product management in marketing research and whomever the project team serves in their own organizations — communities, potentially up to C-level decision makers or other leadership, and the general public.

Some readers of an earlier version of this book read this as recommending insincerity and manipulation, which boils down to dubious ethics. But no, I am being both literal and theoretical when I urge moderators to think of focus groups as theater. Literally, as I have just stated, doing moderation is a performance in which you simultaneously act the part and run the show. That's the functional reality of doing focus groups. For me, it's exhilarating. My first college major was theater and being a focus group moderator gives me an opportunity to enact those roles.

Theoretically, this fits with what is known as the "dramaturgical perspective." As Shakespeare put it in *As You Like It:* "All the world's a stage, And all the men and women merely players; They have their exits and their entrances, And one man in his time plays many parts . . ." Sociologists and social psychologists have taken this metaphor to heart. Many of us analyze life from the perspective of role theory, in which we look at human activity in terms of people acting out socially constructed and defined roles such as mother, father, boss, computer programmer, YouTube personality, fan, and focus group moderator.

The late Erving Goffman, whom I have already cited several times, took this further to suggest that we look at all of social life as theater (that's the meaning of "dramaturgical"). One thing bothered me about Goffman's writings — they seemed to suggest that what we do is "only a role," in the sense of self-conscious play-acting for purposes of manipulation. So I once cornered Goffman and asked him right out if that was, indeed, his perspective. (For the record, Goffman looked kind of like a slightly melted Woody Allen.) Goffman responded that no, it was only an analytic strategy; by looking at human behavior that way — what goes into the "theater" of everyday life in terms of roles, performances, interactions, impression management, and so forth — you could better make sense of what goes on in our everyday lives. Like Goffman, then, I use the ideas of role and performance as a way to understand and communicate what we do in focus group research.

Key performance attributes

Thirty years of experience has taught me that there are four key performance attributes or characteristics the master moderator brings to depth research, which are largely similar to what you would see from a master-level stage actor.

Moderator Attributes for Mastery

Focus

Perhaps the single most crucial characteristic of an effective depth research moderator is the ability to focus attention with beamlike intensity. On one level, you have to be there 100 percent for the participant(s) and the session. You want to be like a method actor, totally in character.

You also need to have or develop the capacity to split your attention without losing that overall, beam-like focus on what's going on. That is, you have to process what you have heard and what you're hearing and seeing; you have to plan your next action — what you will say, what you will do, and how; you have to scan and read the participants; and you have to keep an eye on your audience. Not everyone is able to do this. The capacity to maintain and split focus is a definite prerequisite for becoming a successful moderator. That's something else a master stage actor does, which nobody in the audience is ever allowed to see.

Three demand situations

There are really three different levels of being focused associated with the demand situations of depth research. Doing individual interviews demands the least ability to split focus but is still demanding, to use the word in its other sense. Moderating focus groups exponentially adds to the level of focus required, as now you have to keep track of multiple actors, keep what they are doing and saying and how they are behaving in your mind, and also manage group dynamics. It's not for everybody.

This capability is stretched even more, in my experience, when you load on the demands of running an online group or interview. Kick it up another power of ten. Now you have to attend to the technology, the various "pods," webcam thumbnails (which are visually more demanding than people in the same room with you), working with the cursor in some cases, as well as attending to the virtual back room if you have one. I suspect that at least some who have adequate focus capacity to be satisfactory in-person moderators will be uncomfortable, or ineffective, moderating online groups due to the amount of focus needed.

While I have not had any real difficulty managing online depth interviews (since that does away with the demands of group management), I do not have any desire to manage online focus groups solo. There are just too many variables, too much technology to deal with such as moving stimuli and polls on and off the screen, dealing with the invariable glitches that will crop up, and also managing the group members' technology. Phone lines will drop in and out, as will webcams. Participants will run out of battery, have problems with their computer, and so on. Someone often has to help them get onto the platform, get their audio and, as needed, webcam working, and handle glitches as they come up.

In my opinion, it is or should be a best practice always to have a team member online with you to manage the technological side of things as well as both participant and observer needs and issues. The Blackstone Group, for which I have been doing online groups using its $(IQ)^2$ platform has made it a norm to do so, and so should you.

Intention

Intention, in the sense of the word we are using, refers to being absolutely committed to making your plan a reality. Call it intention or "will," leave no space (or possibility) that participants can or will not cooperate, follow cues or directions, that exercises will not work, that they can or will not play along. Exude confidence. I mean it. The master-level moderator has to present him or herself with total confidence as an act of will. You might have to psych yourself up or even, at times, fake it but you need both to enact total confidence in what you are doing and to actively intend that it will be so. Leave no room for anything else. No waffling, no hesitancy, no suggestion of uncertainty. Method act your role — it is your group or interview and you own it.

It is for this reason that, unlike some moderators, I prefer to just get into it without a lot of explanation regarding such things as the fact that I may push participants to respond or move on, or how I will run the group or interview. I just provide the basic rules of engagement and then begin asking questions and moving along. It's the old Star Trek, "make it so" attitude.

This is particularly crucial when you are pushing individuals outside of their comfort zones. You don't want to give them either cues or opportunity to become self-conscious and begin to question or censor themselves, or stand back behind their faces and try to manage impressions. Just ask your questions, conduct your exercises, and give off that certainty and confidence that they can and will do it. It's your show.

Using another metaphor, you're the hypnotist and they are your subject(s). Coach them as you must, but almost tangibly, expect them to follow your suggestions. Act like it's inevitable, as if it's only natural and expectable. That's how I get interviewees and even group members to engage in guided fantasy, as I described under *advanced tactics.*

Flexibility

A master-level moderator is flexible and adapts to whatever happens rapidly and unhesitatingly. As I have mentioned elsewhere, and will continue to mention, Murphy's Law applies to depth research. Clients' objectives and desires will change. Glitches will crop up. The unexpected and unplanned will happen. You can bank on it.

So a depth research practitioner needs to be flexible. While you might still plan a replicative approach, for example, you need to be prepared to take another approach. It's not so much "go with the flow" as, literally, "deal with it." Adapt. Be willing to create a Plan B, Plan C, or Plan D. Be prepared, like a Scout. Jury-rig a solution, like a MacGyver if you must. Sometimes this means a thoroughgoing rewrite, sometimes just a minor fix.

As a freshman at Antioch College, decades ago, I took a co-op job on stage crew at Studio Arena Theater in Buffalo, New York. I had the great fortune to work with some of the reigning masters of the acting craft, like Jason Robards, Colleen Dewhurst, and George C. Scott. So someone missed their cue, so a piece of scenery came out at the wrong time or ended up in the wrong place — they dealt with it, matter-of-factly without missing more than a beat or two, adjusting their performances, temporizing or improvising as necessary, and the audience (unless they had memorized the play) was none the wiser. That's what you need to do as a moderator.

Unflappability

The corollary to flexibility is unflappability. Don't get thrown, or at least don't show it. Keep your cool, take it in stride — whatever it is. Just act as if it's all under control and keep the momentum going. That's what I saw those giants of the American stage do. This is critical for the moderator, as well.

Perhaps my best example of how stuff may come up that requires you to be unflappable, keep calm and deal with whatever is going on as if it's no big deal happened when I was conducting in-person focus groups with ALS (amyotrophic lateral sclerosis or "Lou Gehrig's Disease") patients. I had already done two groups in different cities with relatively healthy patients. Then came my Houston group. Virtually everyone in the group was in a wheelchair and had come with a caregiver. Okay, no problem, that's ALS.

About midway through the group, the ex-cowboy on my left suddenly started having breathing problems. A ventilator alarm went off. He started gasping. His caregiver, who happened to be his wife and a nurse, jumped up and started trying to clear his airway with something that reminded me of a turkey baster. In my mind, I'm going, "Please don't die on me! What do I do if a focus group participant dies? Please don't die on me!" But I kept my composure, just paused the group and smiled as calmly as I could. Pretty soon the alarm stopped sounding and he was relating how his four-year-old son would play with a lasso in front of him to make his Dad happy. Actually, you could barely understand what he was saying but his wife translated. Whew. What do you do if someone drops dead during your focus group? I still don't know and don't want to find out.

Three basic role choices

Moderators generally employ one of three basic role strategies when conducting depth research.

■ Moderator Role Variations

The Naïf	The Pro	The Insider

The Naïf

The first role a moderator can enact is that of the Naïf. Such a moderator indicates (verbally or nonverbally) that he or she is there to learn from the group, presenting oneself appropriately. This role tends to be used primarily when dealing with technical subjects, in business-to-business, healthcare research, or when group members are older, or hold conspicuously high statuses or positions. It is also highly appropriate for many applied contexts such as community or public policy studies where the goal is to encourage participants to share their needs, hopes, concerns, issues, and other realities while making them feel more like valued, active partners in the project than "research subjects."

The naiveté is, or should be, only an act. The trick is to take a one-down position and come off as intensely curious about what group members have to share but personally unknowledgeable, while using your skills and knowledge to draw out participants and get them to explain "how it is" to you. This role is best adopted by moderators who are willing to act the part and who look the part (i.e., typically younger researchers).

The Pro

The next role is that of the Pro. Here, one straightforwardly does the job of asking questions, getting answers, and probing. One plays it as a professional, a process expert, but not a content expert, much like the role of the "moderator" in political forums, television-news talk programs, or a group facilitator in other settings. Those taking the facilitator role generally share as little as possible about themselves. If possible, they vanish into the group process. Novice moderators are well advised to start by adopting this persona, but many seasoned practitioners use it to good effect as well.

I must admit that, while I often take this role (I stink at playing the naïf) I commonly share more of myself than do others. As I will discuss, I think this helps build rapport and humanizes the event, encouraging group members to be more "real" and candid, but that's just my personal perspective and not necessarily shared by other moderators or clients.

The Insider

The third role is that of an Insider, an expert or at least peer of the group members. This is diametrically opposite the naïf role. To pull this off, you must either be an exceptionally good (and glib) actor or have intimate familiarity with both the subject matter and the everyday life or work world of the respondents. The trick is not to assert insider status (which is likely to prompt resistance from group members), but to enact it matter-of-factly. It is often wise to start by just dropping insider terminology in a matter of fact manner, framing your probes in a technical way that clearly signals you know the field and you understand "where they are coming from." As the group proceeds and you build up that sense of being a peer, you can simply start using the language and terminology of an insider (as appropriate) and digging more deeply from there.

Professional and technical respondents often appreciate this approach, warm up to the moderator, and reveal insights and information that they would not think to mention to a learner or outsider. It helps to look the part, such as dressing similarly to your respondents. Older, more seasoned moderators may naturally gravitate to this style, which helps break down barriers between group members and moderators who look older and more seasoned or professorial. While moderators using other roles can obtain a similar level of disclosure, those who can use the insider role can do wonders in technical areas, working with experts and thought leaders, and getting participants to forget they are in a marketing research event and just "talk shop."

On the other hand, this can be off-putting to some group members who can clearly see and hear that you are not one of them due to age, ethnicity, signs of socioeconomic status, lack of "insider" knowledge, language, or knowhow, or simply because you are clearly an outsider. Consequently, this role may not be appropriate in some consumer, employee, or highly technical professional group settings. In such cases, or if you notice any pushback in this regard, it is best to revert to being a Pro.

Other role dimensions

A related role or performance dimension, is how smart to be (that is, to act). Those taking the Insider role naturally tend to present themselves as being at least as smart as anyone in the room. This can backfire and alienate some people. Just as with the Insider role generally, coming off as too smart (or thinking you're smarter than group members) can alienate some group members. It's a delicate balance, but in my experience taking on this persona enables you to get professionals and other higher-status group participants to think a bit harder and dig a bit deeper than they might otherwise.

On the other end of the spectrum, you don't want to come off as slow to the uptake, but many highly successful moderators play their role as "not the smartest person in the room," bright, but not threatening. Essentially, they want to be able to follow along, understand, and learn from the group.

Again, this is a matter of personal style, comfort, and experiential learning. It is perhaps wisest to start somewhere in the middle and find what works best for you.

A third dimension is how aggressive you want to be. Some moderators prefer a softer, gentle, facilitative, collaborative approach, using judo strategies whenever possible to get participants to open up and play along. Others are harder-edged, more confrontational and demanding, challenging group members who contradict themselves, pushing them to play along. They'll use the equivalent of a karate kick when necessary to keep participants in line and get them to respond. Both of these polar approaches and any number of variations in-between can work. It depends, again, on the moderator and what the clients can or will accept.

Jokes and humor

One last point to consider is the use of humor by the moderator. Sometimes a joke can defuse tensions, create rapport, and help participants to open up. Humor can definitely grease conversation and interaction, if well handled. However, be very careful about jokes and humor in general. The moderator needs to avoid any possible misinterpretation, any sense that one is being a smart-guy or appearing to put someone down. This includes cultural and social-class-related misinterpretations. Some moderators are just good at incorporating jokes and humor into their performance, others less so.

You must never forget the back room. This is where things can really go wrong. For instance, many years ago I cracked a joke to a mixed-gender focus group of obstetricians whose cell phones had started going off (despite the facility's asking them to turn off their mobile phones or at least put them on silent ring). I quipped, "Gee, it seems that as many women go into transition (the last state of labor, when the physician is normally called into the hospital) during focus groups as at four in the morning." It is a running joke among childbirth professionals that babies tend to come in the wee hours. The idea was to get them to laugh as well as to imply that they should only respond to truly urgent cellphone calls. Anyhow, a few chuckled (granted, it was a pretty lame joke), but my client took great offense. He interpreted the joke — something that anyone knowing anything about childbirth would understand — to be patronizing, saying that the women obstetricians were having a hard time transitioning from the office to the focus group. The client called my boss and, on the spot, fired me off the job. Live and learn. Ever since that time, I've been extremely cautious about making jokes.

CHAPTER 10

Session Design Principles

The moderator works with a topical or discussion guide as discussed above. At this juncture, we should open that "black box" to consider some of the basic design principles that can make or break your focus groups.

The kick-off meeting

Before actually moving forward with a project it is customary to conduct a kick-off meeting with your clients, in-person, by telephone, or online. Typically you go over their proposal and ask the project team to elaborate on the reasons for doing their research, the business or other decision that will come of it, and to approve, modify, and help flesh out your research plan.

If possible, you do that old "Vulcan mind-meld" to get inside your clients' heads, and, extremely important, get them to update you. Time and again, you learn that clients have moved on beyond what they originally asked or told you, learned more about their needs, situation, market, capabilities, or situation, modified their goals and objectives, redefined targets, products or concepts, had changes in their team, or changed their timeline.

Functionally, it is important to take this opportunity of interaction with the client team to finalize and get sign-off on the details of your research plan, from the who, how, when, where, and how many to the roles and responsibilities of you and other team members. Among these and other things, this is the time to agree on a timeline and reporting details. This is an essential step both to finalize your plan and to get that all-important client sign off.

Finding participants to recruit

First and foremost, you need to assemble the right people in order to stage a successful event. We have discussed in overview some of the principles of planning group composition, but where do you find these people? There are at least four principle sources used to find a depth research sample.

Qualitative recruitment agencies.

There are a great many recruitment agencies and professional recruiters that specialize in recruitment of qualitative research subjects, along with independent recruiters. Recruiters work with a variety of sample sources including their own internal lists or "panels." Most can recruit consumers, professionals, and businesspeople although they may not necessarily be able to find focus group participants in all regions (particularly outside major metropolitan areas), or with very tightly defined recruitment criteria and may also be weak with respect to lower socioeconomic and minority individuals. However, there are some organizations that specialize in recruiting specific groups, such as Hispanics, or in a specific industry such as healthcare.

Recruiters typically do the recruiting and scheduling for you. While not cheap by any means, the better qualitative recruitment agencies are assiduous with respect to ensuring that they get you precisely the quality of research subjects you want, ensuring that they are not over-researched ("professional respondents"), and will work with you to ensure a good outcome.

Commercial opt-in sample panels

Although largely focused on quantitative marketing and market research, there are a number of panel providers, organizations that maintain enormous panels of vetted individuals who are willing to participate in research. Most focus on consumers although they usually maintain lists of businesspeople and professionals as well. Some specialize in a particular industry, market, or domain, such as healthcare. Some maintain international panels, U.S. only, or for a specific region or country. Panel providers commonly maintain some data on their members' demographics, medical conditions, occupations, etc., but tend to be light on lower socioeconomic status and minority panelists. A few offer "self-serve" sampling, but virtually all will have someone who will work with you one-on-one.

Some will help you find depth research participants and help with recruiting and scheduling, unless your own organization would prefer to recruit, in which case they provide lists of names and contact information. While these tend to present the lowest cost per participant compared to specialized qualitative panel providers, their panel members are typically oriented toward participation in quantitative surveys and their systems tend to be rather impersonal and technology-driven. In addition, they may not have many suitable individuals in any specific area, particularly outside of major cities.

Client and third-party lists

Commonly, your clients will be able to provide lists of individuals from which to recruit "their" groups or interviews. These can be membership lists, customer lists, lists of contacts, or even third party lists they have already acquired.

In some cases you can reach out to third-party organizations or associations to obtain lists of potential contacts, such as membership lists, professional or business directories, lists of attendees at conferences, voter lists, or individuals who have signed up to support a group, charity, political organization, or other cause. There may be a charge for such lists along with various strictures and rules regarding their use.

You can also recruit from telephone and similar directories, although the declining number of individuals and households with landline telephones is greatly reducing their utility. Lastly, there are public domain lists such as voter registration lists, which may be valuable or necessary for obtaining participants in community or other public-oriented research.

Research facilities

Another route is to contract with the facility to recruit your groups. They normally have large databases of potential recruits, from consumers through professionals and executives. Many facilities actively promote signups to their panels on their websites, to depth research attendees, even online. Most will provide recruiting services even if you are not using their facility or other services. Local research facilities know their area and its quirks far better than outsiders, for example travel and timing issues for participants working or residing in what seems to be their coverage area. In fact, their websites sometimes tell you from where they tend to recruit group members.

As facilities join up into larger networks, they gain the capability of recruiting nationally or at least outside their local areas. A good example is Schlesinger Associates, that has grown from a single one-room facility in New Jersey into a global organization with over 20 facilities and which can provide both qualitative and quantitative recruiting services around the globe.

Commercial list providers

There are also many commercial list providers, organizations that specialize in assembling and providing lists of names with contact information from which you or your organization can recruit. List providers may specialize by region, industry, or type of contact; for example, I have dealt with a list provider that specializes in patients with rare diseases and another that claims to have a continually updated directory of contact information for decision makers in the world's energy industry.

These may or may not be separate organizations or lists from those used for telemarketing or direct mail. While they can often provide large numbers of names at a very reasonable cost, the quality of those contacts varies dramatically. For example, the lists may be old and outdated, telephone numbers and emails may no longer be valid, and the names on the lists may or may not be "good" in the sense of being who or what they are supposed to be. Nevertheless, commercial list providers remain an important resource if you have the capability to recruit depth research on your own or in-house. Sometimes they are the only way to find the target audience you are looking for and, in fact, professional recruiters may themselves use such lists. The growth of digital technology has, additionally, created new recruiting channels.

Social media

Today it has become feasible to find and recruit depth research participants through social media such as Facebook, LinkedIn, Twitter, Instagram, Reddit, and so forth. I was probably one of the first to use social media to recruit focus groups and interviewees. I started off decades ago when I was working in the area of multiple sclerosis and put out calls for patients to participate in my depth research on CompuServe's MS forum. Shortly after, I also recruited herpes patients with experience with various therapies through AOL groups. I suspect some of the recruiters and facilities I have worked with are currently recruiting people to be on their panels through social media.

Online communities

Increasingly, organizations ranging from commercial brands and companies to utilities, nonprofits and institutions such as hospitals and hospital systems are forming online "communities" of individuals who can be contacted for research. Access is typically limited to research on behalf of the sponsor but can efficiently supplement or replace traditional in-house lists. While I have not personally used communities for qualitative research, I have conducted a number of quantitative studies using this resource.

Let's assume that you have recruited successfully (we'll consider more aspects of this later) and enough of your recruits have shown up, in-person, online, or on the phone call for you to conduct a group. What do you do with them? What do you put into the discussion guide?

The screener

You need to select depth research subjects properly, and the usual method is using a screener. This is a brief questionnaire that determines if prospective targets meet the desired participation criteria for your study.

Different research suppliers and field agencies tend to have their own preferences with regard to the details. Writing the screening questionnaire is a craft in its own right, and is essentially identical for qualitative and quantitative research and lies outside the purview of this book. (See *Questionnaire Design for Business Research*, 2010, Tate Publishing)

Crafting your discussion guide

Back to the researcher's central tasks. Once you have developed a research plan that involves focus groups or depth interviews and have obtained client buy-in, you need to craft a suitable discussion guide or guides, just as you would craft the survey questionnaire for a quantitative project. The discussion guide will reflect the choices made in developing your research plan, essentially serving as the tool by which you implement it (or at least the data collection portion).

As an example, here are the first sections of actual discussion guide I used for in-person focus groups with mothers who had recently attended some kind of family entertainment with their 4-to-12-year-old kids. This one was essentially a topical guide. If you are following a true scripted approach, you would put down the words you plan to say, although, in practice, most moderators will vary that at least slightly.

Topical Guide: Family Entertainment Moms

A. Introduction and orientation (5 minutes)

1. Explanation of purpose of project to get parents' feedback about live family entertainment
2. Disclosure of recording, listeners, etc.
3. How to participate in a focus group
4. Participant introductions
    a. About their family — number and ages of children
    b. What they and their spouse, if any, do for a living/or are they stay-at-home mom?
    c. Where they live (How long? Native or transplant?)
    d. Spending more, less, same amount of time with family/children vs. 2-3 years ago?

B. Family Entertainments (20 min)

1. Explore what family entertainments they have considered doing/attending over the past few years, whether or not they actually attending (list on <u>flipchart</u>, with hash marks for number who indicate each)
    a. Explore patterns and underlying "whys"
    b. As appropriate, how did they find out about these? (e.g., TV, radio, print, internet, word of mouth, mailings, other)
    c. Which did they ultimately do/attend with their families (note on <u>flipchart</u>)
        1) How often did the do/attend each one listed (note on <u>flipchart</u>)
2. Explore patterns and underlying "whys," probing for their own and their kids' responses (and differences by age, gender, etc.)
    1) What was the process by which they decided to attend each of these (probe regarding the system — who first brought up the idea, how was the decision made, who were the influencers, gate-keepers/gate-slammers)
    2) If not already covered, role of mother, father (if any), children, other family members, friends, etc. (probe extent to which each contributed to the decision, extent to which they were influencers, gate-keepers, etc.)
3. What other things compete for family time?
4. Given opportunity to experience a family event do they prefer weekends/weekdays matinees/evening performances?

Although not strictly necessary, I have come to show estimated time for each section on my guides. Going back over the guide and estimating time helps you check that the design is reasonable for the available time slot. The time estimate can be useful during a session to keep things more or less on schedule, but, most of all, it tends to assure clients and project team members that the session is properly thought out and their needs will be met.

Additionally, depending on the client, you might want to add a one-line statement of the purpose of each section immediately below your section header, generally in a different font. For example, for section B above, I might show: "Purpose: understand moms family entertainment experience and attitudes." This is entirely for the clients; it helps them understand the purpose of the section and, again, feel assured that their objectives will be met. It also helps them obtain buy-in or sign-off from internal clients less familiar with the depth research process. For readability, I suggest using a sans-serif font like Arial.

The discussion guide always begins with an introductory section, a prologue so to speak. This relatively brief module welcomes participants, introduces the moderator, often her or his company, and identifies the goal of the session. We should note that on occasion this is done in a nominal fashion or even one that throws out a "red herring" to cover up the true objectives by focusing on some innocuous or noncontroversial part of the objectives. As my father used to say, in business it is important to "tell the truth, nothing but the truth, but not necessarily the whole truth." The introduction also states the ground rules (e.g., if a group, that everyone should feel free to speak openly when they have something to say, don't talk over one another, that there are no right or wrong answers, and anything they say will be kept confidential and never attributed to them, personally).

Here is where participants are notified about being observed and recorded and pertinent legal or regulatory issues are covered. For the depth research "newbie," it is also useful to explain what will happen in somewhat greater detail than suggested above. While this may be truncated or even omitted for one-on-one interviews, it is standard for groups. These "how tos" are particularly important when starting off an online group, as few will be familiar with the platform, when and how to speak or keyboard, and so on. I usually ask if anyone has done focus groups before and, even if a few have, review the basics (above) and then briefly explain how to use the public chat box, that we will pop up some polls, but that I'd like them to talk just as they would in an in-person group. I often use the metaphor of a Friends' meeting – speak when the spirit moves you.

While you might inquire into the individual interviewee's background at this point, that's optional. In a focus group, the moderator almost invariably now shifts into group members' personal introductions, often asking each to answer some background questions relevant to the topic of the group (e.g., about themselves, their family, their work, personal experiences, interests, work or business). For online groups you might also show them a sample poll and how to compete it (which can be as simple as "how is the day going?" or "which day of the week is this?"). Some of my colleagues doing online groups put up a game in the stimulus box in which each group member can play with virtual magnetic letters once they have "checked in" to the group, even before we start the introductory portion, as a way to make them comfortable with the platform.

The way that you take the group through these first few minutes is a critical training exercise that establishes roles, implicitly (usually) guides subjects in how to respond, while simultaneously introducing them to one another (and to the moderator and observers) as well as establishing the focus of the session. That is, the moderator uses the kick-off module to establish the group as a focused, functioning social system — and to do so within the first few minutes. "Focused" is used in the original sense here, meaning that the discussion is kept on-topic; this is not an unstructured conversation or peer support group. "Functioning social system" means a set of roles, rules, and relationships that hangs together as a whole. In other words, you are training this bunch of strangers to participate constructively and unselfconsciously as a work group. Making that happen is one of the skills of an effective depth research moderator and is greatly facilitated by a well-designed guide.

To blind or not to blind sponsorship

You can recruit and conduct depth research either "blinded" or "unblinded" with respect to revealing sponsorship of your study. Whether to reveal sponsorship of the depth research is an important research design issue. Just as when doing surveys, revealing sponsorship can be problematic in commercial marketing research, but also political, policy-related, legal studies or any study seeking to understand how respondents think and feel about the sponsor and its real or imagined agenda, products, services, or policies. If you and your client (ultimately whether or not to "blind" sponsorship may be up to them) choose not to reveal sponsorship, I typically tell the interviewee or group that we are a research organization looking into the topic, yadda yadda yadda.

Why is this a concern? You may bias the discussion by getting some group members to implicitly manage their responses in such a way as to "take the side" of the sponsoring firm, organization, or whatever, or, conversely, prompt negativity, resistance, even non-cooperation if interviewees or group members are opposed to the sponsor or its offerings. That can turn a focus group into a futile "venting" exercise. Or you can waste precious time and distract from what you are trying to find out by unleashing diatribes against them.

On the other hand, there are situations when revealing sponsorship can positively facilitate cooperation and success or, at least, have no negative impact. This is generally the case when working for or on behalf of nonprofits, associations, nonpolitical and noncontroversial community groups, educational institutions, and so forth. It is almost mandatory when doing employee research and only logical for community and policy studies.

While blinding the sponsor of research may be a pragmatic option, some may call it out as unethical. My personal take on this is that it is not unethical as long as you reveal the topic of the study and, perhaps, what you are trying to find out or what the results of the research will be used for. This is a longstanding practice in quantitative and qualitative research.

Where I, personally, draw the line is at taking on a project in the first place that I believe is unethical or will be used to unethical, distasteful, or otherwise "wrong" ends. Where you draw the line is up to you. I was very uncomfortable, early in my career, when I was assigned to a focus group project for a pharmaceutical company for which the objective was learning how parents could be encouraged to ask for their children with ADHD (attention deficit hyperactivity disorder) to be treated with a product that was actually pure methedrine. Had I been more established in my job and profession, I would have probably turned it down, as did the president of my current firm when asked to do research for a company that offers very high interest loans (to the point of being predatory) for people with poor credit.

A caveat about complexity

One acronym: KISS. Keep it as simple as you can. If anything, I personally tend to overthink and over design depth research, so I suppose I should take heed of my own advice! In any case, review your discussion guide and see if there is any way to simplify or streamline it further. More complexity means more potential for something to go wrong.

Funneling: the basic flow structure

The basic logic of inquiry within the depth research guide is to start with the general and funnel down toward increasing specificity. After the kick-off module, the substantive portion of the guide typically starts with the most general inquiry, e.g., current market landscape, overall situation, or something else that is general, non-threatening and non-controversial, establishing a context for discussion while simultaneously continuing the training and role-setting process. Then move into a more tightly focused, but still general discussion of key issues or questions subordinate to the most general one. After that, step down to yet more finely grained topics.

There is, almost never a single line of flow. For instance, from an overall exploration of the market landscape, you may wish to branch out to several key topics that are essentially parallel, at the same level of generality and priority. You might think of these as individual modules and explore each with a funneling process.

More precisely, the flow of discussion, overall and for each module, funnels along at least four tracks, usually simultaneously:

- From broad to more tightly focused, from the general to the increasingly specific or detailed
- From "safer," easier, less controversial to more edgy, difficult, or controversial
- From the past or present to future
- From known/familiar to unknown/unfamiliar

This approach not only extends the training function, but it makes practical sense. You want to start out with the safe and familiar and then gradually draw out the interviewee or group to discuss more and more specific, challenging, and unfamiliar topics. For example, you might have participants tell their stories (e.g., in a study about products: about their experiences with a product, or how they went about buying something, and what happened subsequently) and then begin probing for more and more specifics. Move on to related topics, then go back and examine key issues with laser focus. First, set the context, for the group members and for yourself, observers and analysts, and then start funneling down from there to the pay dirt.

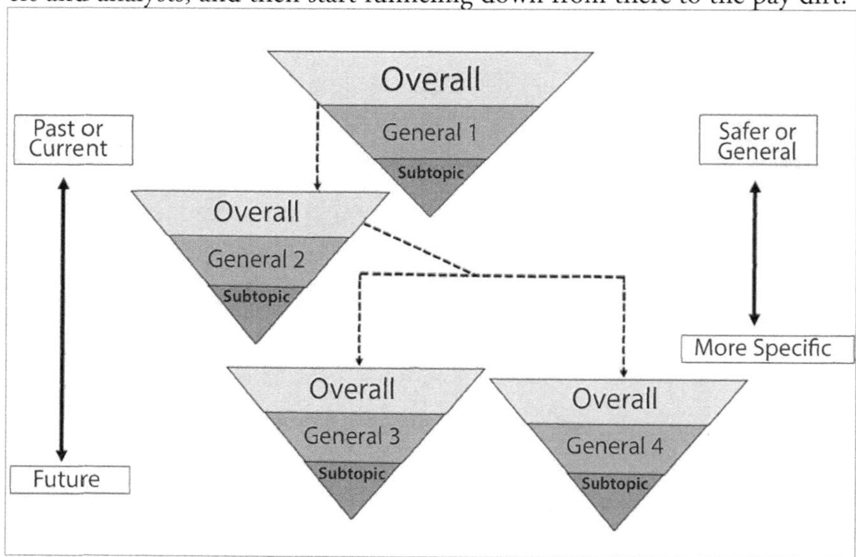

■ Guide Flow Example

Changing things up

Even when you are following the replicative approach, very commonly, the project team will want to modify the guide after the first session or two. What seemed sound on paper may not always work out as well in practice. However much the team has scoured through the guide to eliminate a-priori assumptions, ambiguities, or ineffective sequences of questioning or exercises, it may simply not work out as expected with a real-life interview or group. Participants may come up with or uncover issues or possibilities that the team had not considered, which are clearly important to pursue further; this possibility of serendipitous learning, of course, is a real benefit of depth research. In addition, you are likely to see a way to improve your questions, phrasing, or probing. There is really no way to prepare for, or to eliminate such occurrences by rehearsals or practice interviews or groups. To some extent, every depth research project will undergo at least some minimal evolution.

Fortunately, this is qualitative research. A quantitative survey instrument must be delivered precisely the same way each time to obtain valid and reliable results. In depth research, it is perfectly acceptable to be flexible, shift, and adapt so long as the changes enable the project team to meet its research objectives. If something is not working out, the expert moderator can and will make changes on the fly, getting the client team's approval later. In an online session, you can often do this in real time using the back-room chat capability.

It is far more important to meet the project's objectives — which, frankly, may evolve as your client processes what is happening in the depth research — than to be a stickler for uniformity, following your original vision, or strictly abiding by what was promised in the proposal.

For example, in one of my projects, the team got together and jettisoned about one-third of the topics identified in our proposal (which directly followed the original RFP). As a result, the groups went far more smoothly and the team's objectives were effectively met. However, be prudent and make sure you get your clients' buy-in before making any such changes permanent!

Preparing additional materials

There is often a wide range of materials that you will use during the sessions. This can include both stimulus materials (such as printed product profiles and other materials, storyboards, or videos), self-completion sheets to capture individual responses during in-person groups, or polls and quizzes for use in the online setting.

Clients or advertising agencies typically provide stimulus materials, hopefully with input from the research team. Moderators are often responsible for developing self-completion sheets and polls. Self-completion sheets may range from printed sheets with spaces for verbatim responses, scales for participants to provide ratings, spaces or boxes for estimating numbers, to brief questionnaires similar in appearance to those used in quantitative surveys.

You can hand these out individually at the proper point in the session, or have them all stapled into a packet, which can also allow the order of some items to be rotated, just as in a survey. Some moderators have participants write their responses on a blank sheet of paper. Others (and I strongly recommend this) use custom designed response sheets, which are easier to work with and to analyze. When doing online depth research, I routinely have numeric or short-answer polls prepared in advance to accomplish the same purposes in an even more user-friendly manner thanks to digital technology.

CHAPTER 11

Doing the Research

Everything is set up; now what do you do? Let's get practical: how, exactly, do you maximize your effectiveness and success as a depth research moderator? Let's go through the process.

Before the actual in-person event

You're doing in-person depth research. Okay, you have set up fielding (that is arranged times, places, facilities, recruiting) and prepared all the materials. Based on my experience and learning from my mistakes, let's consider the things you need to cover before actually starting the first interview or group in a series. It makes sense to break this down into two parts:

- What to do before you get to the facility (or other location in which you will conduct the groups)
- What to do when you first arrive at the venue

The following is a series of detailed checklists and tips regarding the items and tasks the moderator needs to accomplish before the actual in-person event starts (with the understanding that SNAFUs will occur). For online research, you can, of course, omit the steps related to travel and the facility, but it is no less critical to have everything prepared and ready to go before you end up discovering that you've missed something. And, as always, to follow the Boy Scout principle: be prepared!

What to do before you step into the venue:

There are often times when you realize you could or should have done or considered something else. I find that I keep learning the same hard lessons over and over again. I won't force you to wade through an all-inclusive, *War and Peace*–length discussion, but let's start at the part of the story where you begin your trip to where you will be doing your groups or interviews, up to the moment you actually step into the facility or other venue. Here are some tips about what to do before you step into the venue for in-person research, followed by a checklist, that may help you learn from my experience:

- **Keep in mind the Boy Scout motto:** be prepared. Leave nothing to chance!
- **Get there early.** Plan to arrive at your destination well in advance of your event so you can check in to your hotel, if possible, or get to the venue early.
  - Be aware of security lines and possible delays when flying, delays if driving or taking a train.
  - Minimize connections if possible to avoid snags.
  - Consider getting TSA Pre-Check or Global Entry status if you travel a lot.
  - Consider relying on carry-on vs. checked luggage to expedite getting out of the airport.

  I suggest that you take similar steps when you are taking a long-distance train or public transit within a city. For example, New York City, has become notorious for subway delays but sometimes that will be faster than getting to a venue by car during times of heavy traffic.
- **Always try to uncover clients' expectations and plans** and be ready to participate in any scheduled or unscheduled meetings. This may require you to modify your own plans. And it applies to online and telephone research, as well.
- **Have printouts of facility and hotel directions with you** when you travel, or have them available on your computer or smartphone, or both if you're a belt-and-suspenders kind of person. Check them before you try getting there to make sure you know exactly where

to go. Even cabbies can get lost and some do not know their way around. In fact, they often ask you what building a facility is in or near what intersection; this is less of a problem with Uber, Lyft, and similar services.

- **Don't forget facility phone numbers.** You can sometimes be stuck outside the facility, with no way to contact anyone except by phone. Luckily, a smartphone will allow you to look it up online, assuming you are not in a dead zone. I suggest having a paper copy with you, just in case.
- **Where to stay when on the road or when flying to your destination:** before an event, stay as close as possible to the facility, the evening before you leave, stay by the airport. Saves all manner of hassles, avoids traffic jams, and lets you sleep in later.
  - These days, I generally choose "second label" hotels like Hampton Inn, Embassy Suites, Marriott Courtyard, Fairfield Inn, Hyatt Place and the like because they are not only cheaper but are likely to have free, grab-and-go breakfast buffets that save time and effort.
  - Be cautious using free Internet service due to security concerns. Many IT professionals recommend using your smartphone's hotspot utility.
- **Use cabs, Lyft, Uber or the like** unless it would be easy to get there by train or other convenient public transit or if a hotel shuttle will take you to your venue.
  - If possible, don't rent a car and drive to out-of-town venues (unless you really like to drive in unfamiliar areas, in which case be sure to give yourself plenty of extra time for traffic problems, road closure, wrong turns, etc.).
- **Always give yourself more time than you think you need.** You never know what will happen next.
  - This includes getting to the facility early, preferably well before any clients are likely to arrive. That not only makes you look good and gives you time to prepare yourself and the work environment, it gives you time to handle any problems that might crop up.

 - Again, the same principle applies to remote (i.e., online or telephone) research.

- **If you're going to be delayed, call ahead** — at least to the facility, usually to the client as well if it will be noticeable to them.
- **Dressing the part is not trivial.** Your presentation will have a definitive impact on your relationship with both clients and respondents.
  - Al Goldman's basic rule was to dress one-step up from your clients; the same goes for your depth research subjects.
  - Generally, business casual is appropriate, but not necessarily, if you are working with professionals or executives in a status-conscious environment (e.g., New York and other East Coast cities). On the other hand, it will probably inhibit group interaction if you overdress for consumer groups, employee groups, groups with children, artists, or "techies."
  - Think of your attire as your costume (remember, it's all theater), and choose accordingly.
  - If you are going to be onscreen for online groups, follow the same principle, at least for the parts of you that will show. I will often put on a dress shirt but keep my jeans or sweatpants on below.
- **It is prudent to travel in your "working" clothes,** unless you will have time and opportunity to change before you get to the facility or other venue. And double check that your attire is clean, unwrinkled, and ready for prime time before you enter the facility. In a recent employee study my shirt had a small stain on it, incurred during my lunch break, I think, but possibly left over from the previous day and a group member complained.
- **Double check everything,** including that you have all the documents and materials you need, before starting the trip and at every critical point thereafter.
  - Be sure to put everything you'll need on your laptop, thumb drive, smartphone, and that means all the addresses, phone numbers, documents, directions, and other files.

– Don't rely on clients to bring it with them or that the facility will always have what was sent to them available.
– Bring everything you will need with you when you when you actually travel to the venue. Your thumb drive or dossier of materials are of little use if they're sitting in the hotel room, and you really don't want to have to run back and get them.
– The same goes for personal items — smartphone, charger cords, tickets, cash and credit cards, driver's license and passport if needed, computer, clothes, personal care items. It is of no use if it's back in your hotel room. That includes your mobile phone.

- **You will undoubtedly forget something** but minimize the chances that you will have forgotten something essential!

To-Do List: Through Arrival at Your Venue

☐ Create your dossier	Print out facility information, directions, at least one copy of all materials to be used in groups, background materials, client materials, etc. with backups on computer, smartphone, thumb drive, etc.
☐ Liase with Project Team	Keep in contact, coordinate and confirm arrangements, keep on top of changes and emergent issues.
☐ Travel preparations	Plan, book travel and hotel arrangements, plan for getting to venue (as early as possible and appropriate before the actual event).
☐ Contact facilities or equivalent	Make sure venue has been contacted, introduce yourself, ensure that materials have gotten to them with instructions and are prepared, check logistics such as flip charts, monitors, food orders, etc.
☐ Pack your stuff	Make sure you have packed your own stuff for travel, then have what you need to bring to the venue with you (double check that all is there).
☐ Dress your part	Come in the proper costume to assert the role you want for clients, observers, group members (and check that it is clean and unwrinkled).
☐ Double check everything	At every critical point, double check that everything is in order and that you have what you need with you.
☐ Get to the venue early	Execute on your arrangements leaving enough time to get there, settle in and set up well before the first group starts and, ideally, before clients arrive.

Arranging seating/seating arrangements

In depth research, even what may appear to be little things count. When doing in-person groups, consider whether you want to pre-structure group seating arrangements. Respondent self-organization is the general rule, letting them choose where they will sit as long as they don't take the moderator's chair, which sometimes happens. Alternatively, you can place "tent cards" with respondents' names on them where you would like each to sit. This can be done to "mix it up" in some way, perhaps break up same-gender groupings, or to strategically place individuals with different work or life roles relative to another. Once again, it's moderator's choice.

Be aware that where participants sit can reflect their personal style or shape their role. Goldman and McDonald (1987), for example, suggest that the person who sits directly opposite from the moderator often takes on a "counter-moderator" role, and may try to wrest leadership away from you. Those sitting immediately to your side may take the role of your helper. Some may try to hide in the corners and minimize participation, which is a good reason to place chairs so as not to create any corners or to use a trapezoidal table that does this automatically. I routinely check that seats are placed strategically to minimize seating that could allow group members to hide behind others or in corners, or to sit in a "privileged" seat immediately to either side of you.

What to do when you arrive at the facility or other venue

Okay, you have arrived at your venue. What now?

- **Stay prepared for problems,** expect them, and handle accordingly.
- **Remember, the facility staff are part of your team.** Make them your friends, treat them that way, and they will go out of their way for you. Too many moderators disregard this, to their loss.
  - The person, who downloaded emails or materials, received a FedEx and other materials, made arrangements with you, clients, or field staff may not be around for your session. It often happens that nobody at the front desk knows where these things are. So ask and problem solve, pleasantly. This is yet another reason why you

should get to the facility early and why you should bring backup materials with you.

- **Usually there is a project folder** and you need to make sure that all needed information is in there and is correct, e.g., whether or what types of recordings to make; how many copies of what should go where; and where they should send or upload recordings, return materials, screeners and sign-in sheets.
- **Make sure that all the materials you will need have been prepared** and prepared correctly and, if not, work with the hosting or other facility staff to get them ready.
  - This includes attendee lists for you and the backroom, stimulus materials, pencils (much better than pens for participants' use during a group), flip charts, whiteboards, and technology, markers.
  - Make sure that pencils are sharpened and markers will mark; too often, some or all will be "dead" or virtually so.
  - If you want papers stapled or clipped together in a certain order, materials printed out in color or in grayscale, check and do what you can to get them corrected. Time and again, I have gotten to a venue only to find that such directions have not been followed. Sometimes materials sent to the facility have been stashed in a back room and your host doesn't know where they are or that you need them now. Sometimes materials are printed in black and white that were supposed to be in color.
  - If you are doing online or telephone research, it is just as important to make sure that everything is ready to go, even if it's going to be virtual. Murphy's law again: if it can go wrong, given enough opportunities to do so, it will.
- **Ensure that materials, including name cards and attendee lists, are literally in proper order.** This includes any that were handed to you by your staff or colleagues to bring to the venue. It's amazing in how many ways things can get screwed up, so check and fix (or at least find a workaround) before your groups start.

- **Name cards are a tricky issue; make sure they are right.** Usually only consumers' first names are shown, and increasingly this is the case for physicians, executives, other professionals. Within your own, your company's, and client's rules for confidentiality, adjust things to your satisfaction. For example, you may feel uncomfortable calling doctors by their first names, and some, particularly foreign-born physicians, may not take kindly to that practice. Also, be sure your own card is correct (or don't use one).

  It generally does not help to assert your own status (having yourself shown as "Dr." if you have a Ph.D. or M.D.) in most consumer and employee groups. However, it can be useful if you have a degree, you are working with professionals, and you want to define your status as parallel with theirs. This might seem trivial, but it is part of role-setting.

- **Double check food arrangements.** In-person marketing research runs on its stomach!
  - It is customary to serve meals to group members participating during meal times, typically sandwiches, but on occasion a complete light meal. Other groups may get the same or just cookies or other "treats." European groups tend to get fuller (and better) meals, even wine or beer sometimes.
  - The project team and other observers normally get full meals. Some like to select these in advance, but it is generally advantageous to let people order off the menus that facilities supply. A few facilities prepare excellent meals, but that is not the general rule.
  - Ensure that arrangements are made before the actual event for you to eat, if desired. At minimum, I like to have a fruit plate available for munching on before, between and after interviews or groups.

- **Check that appropriate beverages are stocked.** Depending on the clients, facility, and location these can range from small refrigerators full of bottled water, sodas and juices, to wine and beer. Many facilities allow you to prepare coffee or other hot beverages on demand, but if not, make sure that coffee is fresh. Don't subject yourself or your project team to old, stale coffee!

- **Check and double check to ensure that everything is set up correctly and is in working order** — the rooms, the food arrangements, and spaces for the anticipated number and types of clients. Make sure pre-screeners and prescreening arrangements (if any), respondent sheets, any releases, are all there and in order.
- **Don't forget to check any technology** (such as computers or monitors), sound, recording, and heating/cooling systems in the focus group and observation room. On occasion, I've had to move my group to a different room because the sound system had failed but nobody knew, which is very disruptive. In at least one case I can recall, the new observation room was stifling hot and the facility could not control the temperature. Try to idiot proof everything!
- **Set-up is very important in the front room.** Set up your props and organize any materials you'll need in the groups, refreshments, water (or other beverages for yourself and group members), pads and pencils (better than pens), flipcharts or white boards, technology, everything.
  - If there's no wall clock in the group room, use a watch or have a clock set up in front of your seat, so that you can follow the time. In a worst-case scenario, have your smartphone out so you can check timing, but then you have to deal with the darned thing "going to sleep" on you.
  - Speaking about smartphones — be sure to remember to silence yours if you have it with you in the front room, and also to ask group members, interviewees, and everyone in the back room to silence theirs as well.
  - Double check that you have everything you'll need at hand, sorted, properly sequenced (especially when you want to rotate order of presentation), and placed where you can reach them in a natural manner. It's a matter of do-it-yourself ergonomics. You don't want to divert your focus to the extra things during the group. With

your attention diverted, it is easy to grab the wrong thing at the wrong time.

- **Organize the back room strategically** and check that everything is in order.
  - Make sure everything works and that you and those in the back room know how to turn the sound from the front room up and down, turn lights on and off, turn on any special lighting for observers, where to plug electronics in, make sure that WiFi and other internet connections work and that everyone knows the passcodes, that refreshments and other "goodies" are set up.
  - Set up "client copies" of attendance/recruitment sheets (usually these do not show last names, while your copies will), guides, copies of stimulus materials, and so forth. Make sure everything is neatly organized where clients and others can find them.
  - Don't forget to make provision for note taking, as appropriate.
- **Don't neglect to check remote viewing and/or recording systems** to make sure they are properly set up and in good working order. After the session, it is too late.
  - As a cost-saving measure, clients today rarely opt to have technicians on hand for video streaming or recording, so you need to ensure that everything is right.
  - Learn how to use the equipment if there are any options, e.g., sometimes you can move or zoom the camera from the back room.
  - Find out where to sit and to put your things in the front room so they do not block video recordings or compromise good sound quality. Share this with your clients and others who will be in the back room when they arrive.
  - If there is a technician, treat him or her like a member of the team and follow their advice. Make sure, by the way, that they get a meal if one is being served.
- **Set up arrangements with the facility staff and clients/observers regarding logistics** such as when to have meals served, which often

includes having clients go through menu books and choose meals an hour or more in advance.
  - Ensure that information gets to the host on when and how to bring participants into the group room, what cleaning and set-up to do between groups or interviews as time allows, how to handle client/observer notes to the moderator.
  - Clarify and share with your back-room team how they can contact facility staff if needed.
- Locate private areas. There are often private areas where you can sit or work away from clients, and where clients can be alone to work or make phone calls. Learn where they are and how they're set up.
  - You may also want to print out your boarding pass or other documents, so, again, check with facility staff.
- **Create an exit plan.** Make it easy to get yourself and clients/observers back to the hotel or airport after the session. Be sure to coordinate arrangements with facility staff before the day the group arrives to avoid delays and embarrassments afterwards.
  - I will never forget the time I was doing groups in St. Louis, Missouri, far from the airport, and a client company's Senior Vice President got extremely agitated (to put it nicely) when the cabbie who had agreed to pick him up at the end of the evening and get him back to the airport for a late flight home didn't show up. Lyft and Uber can help avoid this kind of thing, but plan rather than suffer.
- **Use whatever skills and rituals work best for you — both to prepare yourself and to relax,** ideally both before your project team arrives and before you step into the front room and start the session.
  - Perhaps consider some meditation or visualization exercises.
  - Here's what I like to do, personally: visualize how you'd want to feel after the end of the sessions, perhaps also visualize yourself in the front room making it happen.
  - I've written a couple of books that while nominally about using self-hypnosis contain a number of exercises you might wish to

adapt for your own use (Straus, 2000a and 2000b).
  - This goes for any kind of depth research.
- **Finally, be prepared to fake it,** if nothing else serves!
  - Be unflappable, remember?

Here's a detailed checklist of things you want to be sure to do after getting to the venue and before your groups or interviews start, much of which you may want to adapt for online and telephone research.

To-Do List: When You Get to the Venue

☐ Introduce yourself	Announce yourself, sign in, meet the facility director and other staff, find out who's who and who does what.
☐ Familiarize yourself	Let the facility staff show you around. Ideally be prepared to show your clients around yourself when they arrive. This includes restrooms.
☐ Check the set-up	Make sure everything is in order. This includes making sure the front desk staff and hosts have everything they need, checking the rooms, seating arrangements (enough chairs? too many?) the food arrangements, expectations (and space for) number and types of clients. Also, check sound, recording, other technology, heating and cooling. Get any problems fixed ASAP, preferably before the project team arrives.
☐ Check arrangements	Make sure that all necessary arrangements are in order, for food and drink, any special needs related to the group (e.g., breakouts, technology, prototypes),materials are properly prepared and ready for use, arrangements have been made for leaving afterwards, etc.
☐ Find, prepare, set it up	Obtain and print out copies of all materials to be used in sessions, background materials, find any prototypes, technology, other physical materials, etc. Sometimes everything is ready for you in advance, often it is not. Double check that everything is there and then make sure it is where it needs to be and properly organized for your use.
☐ Organize logistics	Make sure you have packed your own stuff for travel, then have what you need to bring to the venue with you (double check that all is there).
☐ Relax and get ready	Before the action starts and preferably before your team arrives, give yourself alone time to go through whatever preparation rituals you prefer, such as your favorite relaxation exercise before the action starts.
☐ Be flexible and proactive	Keep on top of changes and emergent events. Do whatever is necessary to make things go right. It is better to err on the side of being proactive than to be reactive and try to fix problems after they have occurred.
☐ Double check everything	At every critical point, double-check that everything is in order and that you have what you need with you.

The paramount rule for success

The paramount rule is simply: do what it takes to facilitate everyone's best experience. Moreover, the corollary to this paramount rule is: aim for no surprises. That is, at least, do everything in your power to make it turn out that way. With this in mind, let's consider some of the logistical issues moderators have to deal with, crossing the time periods from before sessions start to the first portions of a group. With only minor adaptation, these same concepts apply to remote as well as in-person groups and interviews.

Getting things started

Now everything is in place and in order and you're ready to start — or are you?

Getting participants there in time

Late arrivals are a big, continuous issue. Even if they have made reasonable arrangements to get to their appointment on time, participants are stuck at work, at home, or in traffic, get lost, miss buses, and cannot find parking; the list goes on and on. The same thing can happen, of course, with your clients, observers, and other project team members.

It is always a good idea to ask recruits to arrive at the facility long enough before your planned start time to allow for any preliminaries such as re-screening, filling out paperwork or self-completion sheets, or just to give yourself a cushion against late arrivals. No matter how well you prepare, stuff happens, so budget your time to allow for starting a few minutes "late," just in case.

Five or even ten minutes before the scheduled start time, it is perfectly appropriate to query staff about individuals who have not yet arrived and urge them to contact recruits to determine those individuals' status, if at all possible. Don't stress yourself out or stress facility staff by nudging them regarding arrivals earlier than that. Usually, professional facilities are proactive about this, but it doesn't hurt for you to take the initiative (and it can calm your clients to do so). This can serve as much for your clients' peace of mind as your own.

I have found that people tend to be slacker with respect to showing up on time for online events than in-person. My Blackstone Group colleagues have found it valuable to ask online group members to log on 15 minutes before the start of their group. We commonly offer an additional, token incentive for doing so (as little as $10). This can really help. If people show up at the nominal start time, say on the hour, it can take many minutes to get them all set up and this starts you off one down with impatient participants and less time for your session than you had planned. Clients can get really agitated about this, as well, which is definitely not good.

How long to wait before starting?

How long do you wait before starting a group without one or more recruits? In addition, what if all or most of the group doesn't arrive at the scheduled time? Alternatively, what if one or more participants call the facility shortly in advance of starting the session to cancel?

Although this is a matter of individual preference and "feel," my practice is generally to delay starting the session no more than about five minutes, if most but not all recruits have shown, ten to fifteen minutes if the majority has not yet arrived, taking into account any cancellations. Then go on ahead. It is prudent to make such decisions in consultation with your clients and observers, but the reality is that "stuff happens." Your ability to control the situation is limited.

A general rule of thumb is to go ahead after the suggested delay, slightly compressing the session as needed to get them done on time and otherwise adapting to the number of recruits who have made it to the facility. You can tell the client that, at least they will save on honoraria!

Individual interviewees, in person or remote, poise a similar issue. How long do you wait until you give up and call them a no-show? It depends on the amount of time you have before the next interview, or whether you have something else scheduled, and how important that particular interviewee is to the project. Sometimes I've waited up to a half hour, sometimes I've felt it appropriate to give up on the person after 10 or 15 minutes. If they are really important and rescheduling is not a good option, I have at times truncated the interview slightly to get them in.

And what if you call for a TDI and get voice mail? Basically, I leave a message that we had an appointment to speak; they must have gotten delayed, and either that I will call again in about five minutes or that we can reschedule (as appropriate). If I have the time, I might try twice in this way.

If a group recruit shows up late, you have several choices:

- **Instruct the facility's host to thank latecomers and just send them home.** This is generally reserved for those extremely late (e.g., more than a half hour after starting time); particularly if they have not called in to tell the facility that they will be unavoidably delayed. We'll discuss whether to pay latecomers shortly below.
- **Have them brought into the group room, possibly after first catching them up or doing so when they enter the front room.** If they have missed important presentations or self-completion sheets, perhaps arrange to have someone from the facility or back room brief the latecomer, show them stimuli, catch them up on any self-completion sheets or the like and then send them into the room. This has worked well for me quite a few times.
- **If not too much has been missed,** have them brought into the room, then spend a few moments summarizing what has gone before, quickly running through the introductory disclosures with them (such as purpose of the group, observation, confidentiality, recording) and bring them into the discussion. This can be a fruitful opportunity to "catch them off their guard" and get fresh information and disclosure not in any way influenced by what has gone before.

If a depth interviewee shows up late, you have essentially the same options already discussed: do the interview or send them home depending on how late, how much time there is before the next interview or you have to do something else. I always try to find a way to get the interview done, even if it has to be shortened, but sometimes that is simply not feasible or the person is so late that it seems to be deliberate or they are just going through the motions. In such a case, it is unlikely that they will be worth interviewing.

Getting the show on the road

Now, let's move forward a bit. Keep in mind that the front room is your primary stage. Remember, it's all theater, at least as sociologists like me see it. Theory aside, taking this approach works. It is wise to make a final check on the group room, to ensure that everything is in order.

Don't however, forget that there is always a backstage, whether in an actual backroom, observers, or listeners to online or telephone sessions, others who may listen to or watch recordings later, and whomever they will communicate with about the research, what went on, and what they learned.

Bringing participants into the room

Leave nothing to chance. Work out a plan with facility staff for how group members or individual interviewees are to be brought into the front room and what you will do. There is no right way. It is a matter of moderator experience and preference. Usually, for example, I prefer to have the host escort group members into the room and give them a minute or two to choose seats, settle in, perhaps interact a bit (as I watch from behind the one way mirror) before I enter and formally start off the session. Others may prefer to escort group members in themselves.

Running the in-person group

I will focus on the in-person group. For telephone and web-based groups, the same principles apply, but need to be modified to fit the context. The same is true for depth interviews.

Make it easy on yourself

First a quick tip, especially for those of us who have aging eyes or less-than-perfect eyesight, I take the final, approved discussion or topical guide and make a "working" copy, double-spacing and using a large font (or at least 14 point). I also like to keep each section or module together, with a new section starting on its own page. This just makes it easier to scan the guide in the middle of doing your group. Oh, another learning from experience: be sure that pages are sequentially numbered. It can be terribly frustrating to find your place if the pages get out of order.

How to use your guide

There is a range of ways for using the discussion guide. Feel free to experiment, modify or hybridize in order to find what works best for you, in general and for your specific project.

As I've suggested, the truly adept and self-confident moderator will commonly glance over the discussion guide as the group starts, then put it down and not refer to it again until the very end of the session, just to make sure that he's covered all bases. This implies the conversational approach, going with the flow, treating the session like a guided conversation. To do it this way, you memorize the topics and flow of the interview, then when starting the group, glance through the guide, put it aside and do not check it again until the very end, to make sure everything has been covered. This approach relies on a mastery of the topic and an intimate familiarity with the topical guide. You should attempt this approach only if you are an expert moderator.

On the other extreme, perhaps the most suitable approach for newer, less experienced moderators is to use the scripted approach and treat the guide literally as a script. You might practice with it a few times beforehand, then read the questions and directions to group members aloud, following the "script" as faithfully and literally as possible. If the group moves on to something covered in a later section of the guide, moderators who strictly adhere to this style will often ask them to "hold that thought" and return the discussion to the point it veered off. "Hired" moderators, particularly in Europe and Asia, tend to follow this style very literally.

Even after all these years, I have my guide in front of me, if only as a kind of security blanket. Like many other seasoned moderators I generally use an approach somewhere in-between scripted and conversational. I keep the guide at hand, literally, checking it from time to time to keep my place, pretty much following the flow as written but making any modifications when and as appropriate. In my opinion, nothing stifles depth research more than literal, linear adherence to a pre-written script.

For instance, if the group gets into a discussion of a topic that appears later in the guide, you let it run as the group is taking it, then pick up where you left off. Using the guide this way allows you to maintain some degree of standardization, helps keep things on track, and permits use of semi-structured techniques while allowing the skillful moderator to depart from the script as appropriate to maximize learning.

It also helps with client management, as many become uncomfortable if questioning strays too far from their expectations, if they don't understand what the moderator is doing, or simply if the flow isn't predictable and linear enough for their tastes. There is always a delicate balance between keeping clients comfortable and "diving deep" into the subject matter with an eye on fleshing out your understandings and analysis.

Starting the session

Okay, now it is finally time to start the group or interview.

- **Notify the facility staff that you want to get started.** Don't expect them to jump at your command, so be patient. Assume they know what they are doing and have a reason for why they do it that way.
- **Make sure that any recordings/remote viewing services are started** or will be started before you start the group process.
- **Be sure to notify the back room,** turn off their lights, turn on their sound, remind them to remain quiet, and so forth.
- **And, away you go . . .** start talking, following your discussion guide.

Wait a second! How did you get into the room? Some moderators like to take their place at the table and have facility staff bring in the respondents. Others (like myself) generally prefer to let group members take their places and get comfortable for a minute or so, perhaps start to interact, then swoop in, sit down and start the group. Doing so allows you to observe the group for a few moments, get a feel for it, so to speak, and kick it off with a bit of a theatrical flourish. I believe that this helps to facilitate group formation and gives the moderator better control over the group process. Once again, it is a matter of the moderator's personal preference.

Coaching participants

The first few minutes of any group are formative, critical to establishing a successful session. The explicit function of this opening part of the session is to introduce group members to one another (and to both the moderator and observers), while exchanging useful information about the participants, the purpose of the session, expectations, rules of the road, and legalities, e.g., client and respondent confidentiality, observation and recording.

In addition, this is the time for what sociologists call the latent function of linking these strangers into a working group. The starting moments of the group, in fact, represent your best (perhaps only) opportunity to establish the optimal role structure and, to be blunt, train participants in how to function as a focus group. This training also allows you to establish rules that will help with practical matters such as obtaining clear recordings, while simultaneously, but implicitly, training clients or other observers as an audience.

In the introductory portion of the session, you work to coach respondents to speak up, speak their mind, but not speak over one another while responding appropriately to the moderator and to one another. For this to be a true group depth interview, not a "serial interview" in which subjects just happen to be sitting around the same table, it is essential to get group members to take turns speaking, but not to speak in turn; that is, you do not want to be "going around the table" in predictable order. While that gives participants a chance to think through their responses in advance, it strips away the quality of group interaction and reduces your ability to surface viewpoints and information that your subjects might not be fully aware of or necessarily wish to reveal.

How, then, do you coach group members? As I've been saying you briefly explain the "rules of the road," in more detail to those who have not previously participated in a focus group. However this may have limited impact. It is best to supplement explanations with modeling the desired behaviors.

Modeling is one of the moderator's best tactics for training the group and shaping members' behavior. Remember that you are taking the role of group leader and setting norms. Act the part you want them to act. In fact, it is often best to overact slightly, for instance, speak a bit more loudly than you would like them to, with slightly exaggerated clarity. And just a skosh more slowly than you would in an informal conversation.

Conducting the actual session

This leads us to conducting the group. Every moderator has her or his own style, but there are some tips and tricks of the trade.

On one level, you are literally the conductor, in the sense of conducting a symphony orchestra. You will not be standing up on a podium and using a baton, but your role is actually quite similar. You are in charge of the performance. You need to bring in each "instrument" at the appropriate time, playing them off against and with each other, modulating their parts to make the whole work; that is, participants' timing, volume, and content. You've got to keep the whole thing flowing, ensure that each section of the conversation goes on just long enough—not too briefly, but not too long to get through the entire "score" and bring it all to a close at the scheduled time.

Some tricks of the trade

I like to keep group members "present" by maintaining a degree of unpredictability. You don't want them rehearsing their responses in their minds, as that will usually get you socially appropriate, prim and proper, surface responses. For example, I like to "swoop," perhaps paraphrasing one group member's response then suddenly turning to another and asking a semi-related question, catching them "off guard."

Of course, if the group is just bubbling up good information, you let that flow until it winds down, perhaps using some of those therapist-like, non-committal expressions to keep it going: "uh-huh," "hmmm," or "yes . . . and?" Another trick of the trade is to be sure to acknowledge each participant's contribution, letting him or her know you've heard and "got" it. A simple, "thank you," often works, or "good," or "fine."

Additionally, it is best to start with more structure and gradually let the group dynamic take over. This can be as simple as calling on people by name when you ask a question or introduce a probe. When you do that, it is best to "mix it up," not going around the table in any routine order but more or less at random. An exception is when a particular topic best applies to a subset of participants, in which case you'd direct your question to one of them, but again, not in any routine order. You want group members to respond when they have something to say, not when it's "their turn."

The same basic sequence and approach works equally well for depth interviews. However, you also need to focus intentionally on creating rapport, just as if you were a counselor or therapist meeting with a client.

Facilitating discussion

Perhaps the two most obviously important skills a moderator must master are (a) getting even the most reluctant individuals to talk, and (b) facilitating group discussion. You do this principally through your own two-way communications with each participant, which you use to both query and probe individual group members and to facilitate interaction among group members. Competent moderators learn to do this, even if they just follow the focus group guide, asking questions and probing appropriately. Nobody likes moderators who talk too much, who fills in the silence with their own voices. However, you can also be too quiet, which is often perceived as being "too passive." All moderators must find their own balance in this regard.

You can also use silence, literally. If you ask a question and nobody volunteers an answer, one tactic is just to look back at the group and wait. Almost invariably, somebody will eventually fill the vacuum and then you're off and running. You might even ask why they are not saying anything and facilitate a discussion about that.

How long to wait is a matter of feel; watch group members, their eyes and body language, and bide your time until you sense that this is no longer likely to be productive. If the "staring game" is getting to you or you think it may be upsetting your client or other observers, you can call on group members by name and ask them the question again. This usually does the trick.

If you do not stop the flow of discussion by acknowledging participants' contribution, but remain silent, you can implicitly encourage them to keep talking, adding to what has been said. In effect, you make them nervous by your remaining silent, and group participants then fill the vacuum.

Open-ended vs. closed-ended questions

One of the most basic tenets of depth methods is that you rely on open-ended versus closed-ended questioning.

Examples of **open-ended** questions (the right way):

- What do you think about XXX?
- Which, if any, of these do you prefer, and why?
- What, in your personal opinion, are the advantages and disadvantages of XXX?
- Why do you say that?
- Tell me more about that (this phrase is not exactly a question but amounts to one).

Examples of **closed-ended** questions (not the right way):

- Do you like XXX?
- Is this the right solution?
- Do you prefer this one or that one?
- Is this an important advantage of XXX?
- Do you mean that you wouldn't find this useful to you?

Open-ended questions and probing allow respondents to structure their own answer in their own way, invites them to explain what they mean, amplify on their initial response and, above all else, does not lead or bias them in any way. This type of question facilitates discussion.

Closed-ended questions restrict the respondents' options, tend to close off discussion, invite yes/no or one word answers, and can lead or bias responses. Even if you eliminate any potential for biasing responses, you are still closing off possibilities. Now, that is fine and proper when doing structured research, qualitative or quantitative. In a survey, for example, you want questions to be tightly pointed, clear, and specific. You normally want to prompt a specific, closed response.

But, in depth research you are far better to err on the side of vagueness or even ambiguity in order to prompt participants to express themselves at length. You want to open up discussion, not close it off or get either a dead-end response or a surface answer.

Some of those who train qualitative researchers see "no closed-ends" to be an absolute rule. In my own experience, however, there are exceptions where a closed-ended question can work. Sometimes it is simply a matter of checking agreement/disagreement. More strategically you can selectively use closed-ended questions to prompt an in-depth response; for example, knowingly asking "do you do this or do that?" with the expectation that at least some group members will come back at you saying "No, we don't do either of those . . ." or "You don't understand, what we mean is . . ."

For the most part, if you just go through your guide, framing open-ended questions for each topic, you can have a very good group discussion and achieve your objectives, with a couple caveats:

- First, you need to dig below the surface.
- Second, you need to get respondents to shed their social "masks"— their presentations of themselves, as they want to be perceived by their peers, by the moderator, by others— and reveal what they really do, think, and feel.

Probing for what, why, how and for more

One of the key benefits of depth interviewing is the depth part; digging beneath the surface. Otherwise, you could get away with the much simpler (and cheaper) expedient of structured interviews. All you would need to get from group members are one word, one-sentence, or yes-and-no answers. Virtually any interviewer could do that, no moderation skills required. However, this would not make for an acceptable focus group or depth interview. You need more.

It is relatively easy to get to the "what" questions. However, arguably the single most important contribution part of depth research is uncovering the "whys" and the "hows." While you can identify relationships and get subjects to reveal preferences and decision-making processes (e.g., relative importance) through statistical methods, surveys will not tell you why people do what they do or at least what they think to be their rationale. While there are any number of quantitative strategies and statistical methods to assess cause vs. effect and even tease out some of the whys, deep understanding of why people do what they do and how they go about it, how they relate to issues and challenges or products or policies, their strategies, motives and motivations, and how these relate to their history, culture, and context, and what it's like for all involved are best discovered and explored through qualitative depth research.

You could train a parrot to be a fairly good marketing research interviewer if, every time a participant says anything, the bird were to say, "Why?"

Of course, you would need to record the responses, make sense of them, and fit them into your analysis. My point is that every moderator needs to make it a habit to follow up virtually every question about the "what" with "Why?" and "How?" "Why do you say that?" or "How do you explain that?" These, however you phrase them, are the most important probes moderators use to follow up substantive questions.

Getting participants to clarify or expand on responses

Depth research subjects are often predisposed to give you easy "vanilla" answers to your questions, no more than a couple words. You need to get participants to talk freely with you and, perhaps more importantly when doing focus groups, to get them to talk with one another about what they think, feel, or do at some length; and, then to respond to one another's points, again at some length. Every moderator develops their own best ways to do this; it's a matter of trial and error and finding out what works best for you.

If you are lucky, participants will do this for you on their own. For example, group members will respond to one another's statements, either supporting or challenging them. You should foster this behavior. Ask them to explain what they mean, why they said what they did. Keep on asking for more, for the "whys," and for "anything else?"

Sometimes you need to push depth research subjects discussion when their tendency is to provide a few brief comments and then stop, waiting for you to move on. One of the simplest tactics is to ask them to clarify their responses, asking them to help you, as an outsider, understand what they are trying to communicate, or to give concrete examples. You can also prompt them to expand on what they have said: For example, "Please tell me more about that" If it's a focus group, you might then invite others to comment on what the first person said.

Summarization

Another tactic that helps you dig below the surface is to paraphrase what participants have said and ask them if that is what they mean. The obvious approach is to try to capture in your own words the individual's perspectives and group consensus (or the perspectives of various segments within the group). Then let them respond and clarify any points you appear to be unclear about, or possibly didn't quite "get."

You can be tricky about this, and intentionally "get it wrong" or incomplete; this can prompt participants to chime in and correct you. Then you can use that as an opening to foster a conversation about the topic, ask them what you should have said, or what they meant to say. By putting yourself in a "one down" position, this can be a sort of judo strategy leading depth research subjects to fall all over themselves to explain, perhaps justify their position, and help you to get it right. I am not suggesting that you engage in duplicity or manipulation — this is a tactic, just like Goffman's use of the "dramaturgical metaphor" to get at how people construct their lives. I learned the value of this tactic, by the way, when I tried to summarize what a focus group was telling me and inadvertently got it wrong. This is a good example of learning from one's mistakes, literally.

Nothing is better than a good argument

Your goal is to have group members forget they are in a focus group. You want them to be so involved in the emerging discussion that they drop their social "masks" and other usual defenses. You want them to say what they are really thinking, reveal what they really do and feel in everyday life. You want them to "get real," in other words. To accomplish this, you want them to take sides, create ad hoc alliances, either try to get you to understand what the world looks like from their perspectives, or to reveal and defend their perspectives to one another.

One of the very best ways to make this happen is to foster what amounts to an argument. A polite, friendly one, to be sure, but an interaction in which group members focus on one another and struggle to get their point or way of seeing or doing things across, take issue with what the others say, try to get others to see it their way.

One of my formative experiences, in my very first focus group, was having this happen spontaneously. As I have mentioned earlier, it was a group of HIV-positive men, very early on in the epidemic when people with AIDS felt hopeless, angry at the disease and at Burroughs, Wellcome & Company, who provided the only drug to treat it. The FDA had just approved the drug for use before an HIV-positive person progressed to full-blown AIDS — such use was the topic of the group. As it happened, several of the men were attorneys who were very knowledgeable and involved with a local community support group. They spontaneously started up a lawyerly debate between those who were favorable to early use of the drug and those who were against it. A lot of very useful, very "real" information came out of that discussion, even more so because a couple of the other group members were younger, knew virtually nothing about HIV and its treatment, and questioned and probed the debaters in order to learn more.

Ever since then, whenever possible, I have tried to get group members to present opposing positions and work it out among themselves, since I've not figured out how to prompt an impromptu argument. At the very least, you might identify group members who have taken very different positions on a subject of interest and say something like, "Bill, you said you agree completely with this proposed policy, while, Sarah, you disagreed with it very strongly. Bill, what might you say to Sarah to get her to see it your way?" (or vice versa). Then get others to chime in. Even more mildly, you can bring out differences in opinion and ask the group about it: "Some of you have indicated that you agree with this proposed policy, while others of you disagree very strongly — why do you think that is?" Or "tell me about it," or even name names ("Some of you, like Bill . . ."). If you get it right, you will almost vanish out of the group members' consciousness for a while as they discuss or confront one another over their differences.

If participants ask you questions

One thing the moderator is not and should never be is an information source, at least with respect to the topics relevant to the research. You want the group members to be the informants; so, what do you do if group members ask you questions?

The basic rule is that you can answer questions about what you mean by what you say, or what you are asking them to do. When it comes to clarifying terms, it gets trickier. If it is a matter of abbreviations or acronyms, or technical language not directly related to what you are seeking to find out, then you can generally address the question. If needed, you can explain what printed or other materials are trying to communicate—for example, if they are worded in a way that the respondents cannot understand.

In such cases, it is a good practice to repeat their query and state, for the recording or transcript, what they are asking about and give your answer. If the question is really one of "tell me what you want me to tell you," or asking for clarification of important terms central to the study, do not give your own answer but ask group members what it means, what they think the answer is, or the like. Do not feed them information!

At the same time, questions will come up that are legitimate and need to be answered for group members to understand what is being asked of them or to make realistic judgments. The best approach in such cases is to pass a note or otherwise signal the back room (or equivalent) and get your clients to provide clarification. This is even easier when doing the group online with a back-stage chat function or the equivalent, during groups discussing technical matters or seeking clarification. After asking participants what they think it is or means, I have commonly received information from the project team that I can pass on to the group to move the discussion forward.

One should, nevertheless, be very, very grudging about giving out additional or background information yourself, doing so only if that is the only way out of a box canyon situation.

Using numbers (correctly)

Another issue that merits at least brief mention here is the generation and use of numeric and other quantitative-type data in focus groups and depth interviews. As I have discussed, while we may occasionally employ sophisticated hybrid designs (qualitative/quantitative) or very large sample sizes that can provide valid statistical data, for the most part we get numbers for one of two purposes. The first is to get a sense of how many, how often, or how strongly, perhaps to explore pricing and price sensitivity. It is completely reasonable and appropriate to do so, as long as you are clear that you are only seeking to gain a "feel," or perhaps an ordinal understanding of where respondents are "coming from" and what they are thinking.

The second reason is to accommodate the client, who is often unclear about the distinction between qualitative and quantitative research. This can be tricky to manage, as they may expect you to report means, or other statistical analyses even for single groups or perhaps two groups held in an evening as part of your debrief. If possible, try educating them on the use and value of qualitative "numbers."

Many moderators play along and give clients the numbers they ask for, either because they are themselves not quantitatively knowledgeable enough to understand the pitfalls involved, or because they need and want to please their clients. The risk is that marketers will take these numbers and "run with them," leading to ill-informed decisions. Sometimes the best you can do is to be explicit that the numbers should be regarded as qualitative and directional at best, but not statistical data. Be sure to make this point clear in the reports you write, as I will discuss in the next section of this book.

Problem solving tactics

As I have stressed, Murphy's Law definitely applies to running focus groups. Anything can happen! Let's consider some of the more common problems one has to solve as a focus group moderator, the things that can cause you to stumble.

Problematic participants

You can normally get virtually any individual interviewee to play along and contribute, if only by giving them no "space" or permission to not co-operate, although once in a very great while you may simply have to give up on a particularly recalcitrant recruit and send them home. On the other hand, one of the issues that crops up regularly in focus groups and is often cited as a weakness of this methodology is varying individual participation levels. Some members do not contribute appropriately to the group and there are others who, one might say, over-participate and those who do not participate at all.

Dominating or obstructive individuals

One of the most widespread critiques of group methodology is that other group members can be influenced by a dominating individual. According to Goldman and McDonald (1987), this type of person commonly chooses a seat directly opposite from the moderator. They may try to take over the group, as a type of counter-moderator, or may "hog the spotlight." In any case, they dominate the conversation and often manipulate the group process, creating a sort of "groupthink" following their lead.

Sometimes this is related to that person's role or status outside the group, a recognized expert or leader, for example. You cannot always screen out such individuals in the recruitment process, but it is best to try.

More often, however, it is a matter of personality or personal style. The dominating person may seek to establish him or herself as an authority figure, whose pronouncements are to be accepted by others, period. Often they are a bit more subtle than that, but this is the underlying message.

Another type of over-participant is the obstructive individual, who just will not "play the game" or "play along." They may refuse to follow the moderator's instructions or requests; challenge the moderator, sometimes with increasing hostility or anger; disparage the topic, stimulus materials, or research process; or sometimes act inappropriately toward other group members (e.g., become critical, impolite, disparaging their viewpoints). While the first type simply dominates the group conversation, this character obstructs it.

In either a case of over or obstructive participation, the moderator can first try a few unobtrusive interventions. One is to skip over the person, calling on other group members by name to answer a question or otherwise respond. If there seems to be a "groupthink" phenomenon emerging leading the group to follow a dominant individual's lead, you can explicitly ask for differing opinions. After this happens a few times, many troublesome individuals settle down.

You can move your intervention up a notch during in-person groups by turning your back to (or at least not looking at) the problematic group member, literally "giving them a cold shoulder" when they do not play along appropriately. Of course, you should then strongly reinforce any positive responses on their part, if only by thanking them for their contribution. This is most likely to help with dominant participants and less likely have an impact with the truly obstructive person.

If that does not work, you can try gently asking them to behave in the desired way, or to act differently. This can be uncomfortable, but sometimes it can work. Perhaps you can think of other tactics, but the final escalation is to cull the person from the group. While just asking them to leave may be too confrontational for most moderators (and is likely to disrupt the group), a common tactic is having someone from the facility pop in and ask the person to come with them, perhaps saying there was a phone call. You might have to duck out of the room for a moment (under some kind of neutral pretext) to allow for this. Then, unless the situation is truly egregious, the host "pays and sends" (see below).

Non-Participants

Another variation is the non-participant. This person does not play along, but in the other direction from a dominant or obstructive individual. These are group attendees who just sit there, staying out of the conversation, or who provide terse, one or two word responses. They often annoy observers and clients who see them as literally a waste, a missed opportunity for a useful participant, and a monetary drain.

You can call on non-participants by name, and encourage them to take a more active role. You can try to encourage overly terse non-participants to complete or explain their thought, and probe them heavily to get them talking. The idea is to encourage or train them to participate actively. You can go on to escalate similarly as for over-participants, if necessary asking them (nicely) to join in on the conversation or activities.

Two of the strengths of online groups are that (a) it is more difficult for a single participant to intimidate others as, for better or worse, you lose much of participants' body language and similar signals, and (b) starting from your introductory comments, you can make it acceptable for shyer or quieter group members to keyboard at least some responses. I will encourage that when appropriate. Nevertheless, you may still end up with some dominating personalities, non-stop talkers and opinion-spouters or individuals who just won't participate.

I must admit that sometimes the moderator can lose track of who is or is not actively participating, particularly in online groups because you have to focus on so many different factors and, especially if they are not using a webcam, it is easy to lose track of who is not doing their part. This also happens during in-person groups, particularly when a lot is going on, discussions are heated, or you are trying to cram a lot stuff into a short time. Try to keep alert to who hasn't spoken in a while or seems to be hiding (sometimes, nodding out if they are tired, bored, ill, etc.). Call on them by name, ask them questions, or ask for their opinion on what someone else has just said. Not uncommonly, your observers may notice such individuals even when you don't and send in notes.

If a group member remains useless, simply "pay and send." Often your clients will ask you to cull them (e.g., send out a note). It's part of the cost of doing business and almost impossible to screen out these types of participants ahead of time.

Pay-and-Send

As the above suggests, occasionally the moderator needs to send somebody home, most commonly from groups but sometimes from one-on-ones. You may have over-recruited (and everyone shows), or they are not working out. Most often, the solution is to pay and send. This term means what it says. Pay the individuals their honoraria and send them on their way. You usually have the facility staff do this for you.

What about those who fail prescreening or are late-comers that you do not want to let into the group? Do you "pay and send" or just send them home without their incentive? There are no fixed rules, so this is up to you and your clients. In this business, we occasionally come across "professional respondents." Good recruiters try to screen them out, as do panels, and we sometimes set an eligibility criterion for how long it must have been since their last group or, at least, last market research event regarding your topic (commonly at least three months, sometimes longer).

Sometimes, you may end up with recruits who try to work the system by intentionally showing up late in hopes of being "paid and sent." Moderators and facilities also become suspicious that some recruits use other tricks, such as arranging for somebody to call them at a predetermined time after the group starts so they can claim there is a crisis and they have to leave. Pay or send? There is no fixed rule. Do what you feel is right given the circumstances. As appropriate, I will first check with the back room, since clients may have to pay for a "dud" who is sent home. About the only defense against such individuals is to have them placed on a "do not recruit" list.

Negative group dynamics

Some participants are clearly "bad recruits," having somehow slipped through the screening process, and have nothing to contribute. Others may prove to be useless, grudging participants, possibly even intoxicated or otherwise incapacitated, giving at best one or two-word answers. Then there are occasional individuals who will not be moderated, try to take over the group or at least dominate everyone else, perhaps not conform to rules of decorum.

Sometimes you discover you have a thought leader, acknowledged expert, or other individual in the group to whom one or more others clearly defer.

In such cases, it is usually best to cull them from the group. The usual tactic is to have the host from the facility enter the room and ask them to step out, commonly under the pretext that they have a phone call. Then thank them, pay them (if you and the backroom deem that appropriate) and send them on their way. This may involve "cooling them out" –as the great sociologist, Erving Goffman put it (1952)—saving face for everyone, providing a rationale reducing any anger, exasperation or indignation, "that makes it easy for him to accept the inevitable and quietly go home."

Even if you do pay and send, that may not be enough to satisfy some people. The author recalls an instance where a physician who was also a highly influential medical school faculty member showed up about 45 minutes late for a focus group in Milan, Italy. The group involved a multi-step process that had already advanced too far for her to join in at that point. Even though the moderator stepped out of the room and tried to cool down the physician, she later contacted the sponsoring company and threatened to boycott them and tell everyone that they had disrespected her. This really backfired on the research team! In retrospect, it would have been wiser to have her briefed, join the group, and start participating at the next appropriate juncture.

You occasionally run into the same issues with depth interview participants. Sometimes they prove to have just been bad recruits, like when you discover that they fibbed about their age or other screening criteria. As appropriate, if they are non-cooperative or unqualified, I'll stop the interview, cool them out, and send them on their way.

Avoiding group-think

I've already emphasized the tactic of getting focus group members to provide individual-level responses before subjecting them to group process. The idea, to recap, is capturing their individual responses before these are shared with the group, in effect getting each person to commit to a point of view before group process can "contaminate" it. Even then, participants will often try to get away with not reading what they wrote but saying something like "I agree with her," whether they do or not. You don't want them to respond as in the movie, *When Harry Met Sally,* "I'll have what she's having."

Consequently, the moderator has to be strict about getting each person to read exactly what they wrote, in order to capture variance and differences of opinion. While this information is valuable in its own right, it has the further benefit of allowing the moderator to facilitate group discussion using actual individual responses as a stimulus.

Managing too-quiet individuals

Some focus group and depth interview subjects are not really non-participants but tend to speak very quietly, sometimes also non-assertively in the sense of minimal statements and responses. In many cases, this appears to be the person's normal personal style. In others, it seems to be a matter of shyness or discomfort speaking out in a group setting. In either case, even if audible within the group room, their hushed tones make it hard for observers to follow and even more difficult for subsequent analysis and transcription from audio sources, DVDs, or other media.

Often the best and simplest strategy is to ask the person to speak more loudly, perhaps reminding them that the session is being recorded and we want to be able to hear and capture everyone's contribution. At the same time, you, as the moderator should make a point of modeling the desired behaviors, by speaking more loudly. Sometimes, to make the quiet speaker more comfortable, it is helpful to say that you, too, tend to speak more quietly than you should be doing and will try to speak more loudly and clearly. If you have prompted them more than twice without success, it is probably best to stop pressing the issue Otherwise, you can lose their participation for whatever it is worth.

Overly tired participants

As I've already noted, there are times when interviewees or group members show up already clearly and sometimes severely fatigued, most commonly in later evening sessions (8:00 or later). On other occasions, again most often during the evening, one or more participants visibly become fatigued as the group or interview goes along. In either case, their responses are muted, their response times are slow, and, their discussion is minimal. You start getting one-word answers. Interaction may threaten to slow to a halt. The backroom may get restless and impatient with you as the moderator.

Obviously, this is not a good situation. There are some interventions you can try with groups or depth interview subjects. Sometimes you can wake up the session a bit by modeling, upping your own pace, volume, or modulating your tone of voice. Moving things along in a snappier fashion sometimes helps. That's about all you can do for remote groups or interviews. Another tactic, which the author learned from an experienced colleague, Morris Whitcup, is to have the facility make the room colder, if necessary, almost to the point of uncomfortable. That can often bring the group or interviewee "back to life and perk things up amazingly. A short structured stretch break can also do wonders. Get everyone on their feet to do a simple stretch and breathing exercise and then get back to work!

What if nobody is willing to cooperate?

One of the thorniest problems you might encounter is when nobody in the group is willing to play along with the program. This can happen with individual interviewees, but it's more often a group dynamics problem.

For example, you might be discussing new products or other offerings. Some group members may prove unwilling or unable to accept such a possibility or scenario, particularly if you are talking about something that is a game-changer or in some other way seemingly incompatible with their present experience. On occasion I've also had group members who balk at cooperating with anything to do with marketing, even though they knowingly signed up for a marketing research event, as clearly disclosed in the screener or invitation. You need to encourage them and keep the session moving.

Just one or two doubters, skeptics, or cynics can infect the whole group with their attitude, or the group as a whole simply will not cooperate. This happens with some frequency when doing marketing research with physicians or other professionals, particularly in some regions like the San Francisco Bay Area or the Northwest, where the medical culture is very strongly "evidence based." But it has happened to me even in Philadelphia. I was conducting a group with medical specialists at my firm's in-house focus group facility regarding a new cardiovascular drug. We got to the central, positioning exercise. Disaster began when one or two particularly jaded physicians (who appeared to be friends) complained that none of the positioning statements was acceptable; they all were "Madison Avenue hype." The whole group then refused to participate in the exercise. The session ground to an embarrassing halt.

At such a juncture, you have to use all your ingenuity to resuscitate the group, perhaps even agreeing that this is, indeed, marketing research and reminding them you have bought their time for the next hour (or two). That has worked for some of my colleagues. You might ask them to take the role of the marketer and, knowing their target audience, they should complete the exercise from that perspective. This last suggestion is a kind of judo tactic that sometimes works better than a more karate-like, confrontational approach.

In the Philadelphia case above, nothing worked. Group dynamics led to textbook group polarization. I couldn't get anybody to budge and saw no option other than to end the group. I lost the client. In retrospect and with the benefit of years more experience, I suppose I might have structured the event as a co-creation exercise, perhaps with some elements of gamification, but in that particular case, the clients had basically handed us the methodology and materials and there was really no option but to follow their marching orders.

Advanced tactics and how to use them

We've already introduced the possibility of using advanced tactics in your depth research. Now let's consider how to use them. Let's start off with two single, time-honored projective techniques that can be used in groups or individual interviews.

You are at a party . . .

One of the oldest of the projective techniques used in focus groups (but which certainly can be used in depth interviews) is to have participants imagine that they are at a party and various products, companies, brands, or other offerings show up, then asking what actor, animal, character, kind of person that product, company, or brand would be. For instance, decades ago when I was first learning to do focus groups at National Analysts, we were exploring the disruptive impact of the Acura Legend on the luxury auto category. I'd ask group members to imagine that they were at a party and a person representing Acura entered the room, then asked them what that character was like. Similar questions were asked about Mercedes-Benz. The Legend generally came off as a friendly, contemporary professional and the Mercedes as a stodgy matron. This certainly told us something about how luxury car buyers perceived each brand!

The "elevator story"

The "elevator story" is another time-honored way to get depth research subjects to summarize their thoughts, feelings, positions, and so forth, and then share these with the group as a means of fostering in-depth discussion. The classic method is to ask participants to imagine that they are in an elevator with a peer who asks them about the product, concept, or whatever is the topic at hand. You stipulate that they only have the few moments until the elevator arrives at the next floor to answer that person, and then have each group member write down their answer. Once everyone has finished, go around the table and have participants read their answers aloud. In an online group, you can use a short-answer poll or even just ask participants to keyboard their responses into a chat box. When they have all completed the task, you can then facilitate discussion around areas of consensus, disagreement, or perceptible segments of opinion.

I commonly vary the set-up, for example, having the group members imagine meeting the other person in a hallway or at a shopping center or store, or in some other likely context in which they might meet a peer. Sometimes rather than a peer, the other person might be defined as a student, a trainee, a subordinate, or a relative—whatever makes sense.

Collaging

Another projective technique that can be used in groups or depth interviews is "collaging." You task individuals or teams to construct collages from pictures cut from magazines or other material to represent the target of the research. This could conceivably be adapted to online groups and either in-person or online interviews as well, using an appropriate tool, and is routinely done with some of the asynchronous platforms currently available.

Projection with images or objects

Another widely used projective technique is to present interviewees or group members with a set of printed images (for instance, a set of paintings in various styles), or even objects and ask them to select the one that most feels like or fits a concept, product, or whatever you are trying to get their non-rational responses to.

When I was teaching marketing research, I once demonstrated projective techniques to my class by gathering a number of little stones and pebbles from my garden and asking the group to choose the one that feels closest to a tiny digital video camera I brought to the group. One student chose a piece of bark dust, saying that the camera is "bogus, not a real video camera at all." Another chose an oblong stone that was very smooth, rounded, and glossy, saying that this is how the camera feels to her. Again, the trick to getting valuable information from such an exercise is probing the "whys" in a group discussion.

A useful "do it yourself" approach is to put together a number of very diverse images and again ask group members to choose the one that best fits how they think and feel about whatever you want to explore. They can be shown together as a composite, as a stack of hard-copy cards or as virtual images. Some research firms have developed their own decks – for example, of various paintings in different styles and colors, or little objects. There are also some standardized image sets available, sometimes at least supposedly calibrated and demonstrated to correlate with specific emotions or other responses. I personally tend to prefer a DIY approach and, to be honest, don't trust claims regarding proprietary, standardized decks with "proven" meaning or interpretations. There are, for example, decks of what amount to emoticons that supposedly represent different emotions, but are they cross-cultural? Do they really convey the same things to everyone? I may be an outlier but they don't work well for me, personally.

Here is a grayscale version of an exercise I used for some central location focus groups that could also be used in the online setting and with individual interviewees. These are photos I had in my computer and more or less randomly assembled. As you can see, they are intentionally diverse and sometimes cryptic. Feel free to use it yourself.

Guided visualization

Guided visualization or fantasy is the most radical projective technique I've used. How I do it is inspired by my experience doing hypnosis and suggestion as a clinical sociologist. I first developed this technique years ago when I was charged with understanding how customers would feel and think about Botox for cosmetic use, its indication for which was still forthcoming. While I have most often used this technique in the in-person depth interview setting, it has also worked with focus groups. For one study, I brought it off with groups of psychiatrists! When I use this technique for marketing research, I have the following approach. Feel free to modify it to your needs and preferences.

Straus guided fantasy technique

In addition to the target concept, company, product, policy, or service, select for comparison one or two key competitors or existing alternatives that your interviewee is already familiar with. Here, let's term the object of our study "Agent X" and the comparators "Product Y" and " Product Z" (in a real session, I'd use the actual names of Product Y and Product Z but not that of Agent X, unless it's already known to the participants by name). Here's how it works:

1. After briefing the participant(s) on the new product, tell them we want to use the power of their imagination and engage in guided fantasy or daydreaming. Tell them you will ask them to close their eyes to shut out the real world, since this allows us to imagine more freely. Say that you're going to say the name of a product and want to explore what they will see in the theater of their imagination. (I like to use that metaphor — you could also use the metaphor of a movie screen, computer screen, whatever). Now tell them that Agent X walks out onto their mental stage. You wonder what it will look like . . . it might be a person, an animal, an object, it may be realistic or cartoony . . . whatever comes into your mind . . . it may start out rather vague or hard to see but it will get clearer and clearer as you watch it in your mind's eye . . . it will take as long as it takes but it will appear and get clearer and clearer . . . (Those ellipses are my attempt to suggest pauses or at least breaths taken.)
2. Give it a minute or so to "develop" and then ask them what they saw in their mind. Repeat for Products Y and Z.
3. Each time ask them to tell you what they see in their mind. Now go back and ask them to recall how they visualized either Product Y or Product Z , describing it in as much detail as they can. When that winds down, begin asking them questions about what

they visualized. Start with peripheral stuff and spiral in toward the central object. You will find that the central figure starts to fill in more clearly and in more detail as you do. For example: where does it live? what does it do for a living? what does it do in its spare time, for fun and enjoyment? Take it as far as you'd like, even down to what kinds of TV shows, movies or books or music it (or he or she, whatever they imagined) likes, who else lives in its home, how is the home decorated? After it all gets pretty concrete in their mind, pounce and ask two questions: "What it is like for you?" and then "What is your relationship with it?" (Feel free to seed with friend, teacher, helper, peer, boss, subordinate, etc.)

4. Go back and, more briefly, repeat for the other comparator. Then remind them how they visualized Product X and go through similar probes in somewhat greater depth. Doing it in this order trains them in doing the visualization and leads to the clearest imaging of your actual target.
5. Now have them open their eyes and come back to their everyday world. That's it. Basically, I have found that by focusing on what's in the background, our minds fill in the foreground. I will discuss this concept of figure-and-ground in more detail below.

Strategically, the idea of using this kind of project technique is to get at how your subjects feel about and relate to the things you are having them visualize, at a deep, even non-rational or pre-rational level. We make sense of the world through metaphors and similes likening what is novel to what we are already familiar with (Pepper, 1970) and this exercise is designed to tap that process. It's pretty easy to get research participants to tell you want they think, but this takes things to a far deeper level.

Most of those with whom I have used this technique find it to be enjoyable, although a few have claimed that they "have no imagination" and are unable to do the task. I have had many interesting metaphors and similes crop up. Witches, Robots, Avis Car Rental (in the days of their slogan, "We Try Harder" when they were number two to Hertz, which was how that person visualized the dominant product in its category). One Hispanic orthopedic surgeon visualized a new drug and the competitors as literally three compatriots from "the hood." Perhaps the most unusual example, from that same study, was a physician who visualized one of the old products as a Gene Wilder character in a canoe, looking kind of like Einstein, very inefficiently flailing away with his paddle, while the new product was a gorgeous young woman in a skimpy bikini who paddled along smoothly with superb technique, and then the physician went on to say "my new wife — umm, that's just what I imagined . . . I'm happily married!" I think you can interpret for yourself what he was saying about the new drug and his likely relationship to it.

Online focus group tricks and tips

In general, you moderate online groups the same way as you would in-person groups, only remotely. While you sacrifice some of the immediacy of the in-person setting as well as many non-verbal cues, using webcams you can at least see facial expressions and create the sense of virtual presence in the same room. If you have a back-stage chatroom set-up, your clients or other project team members can observe at least as well as they would from a physical back room.

When working with an online group platform like the one discussed earlier, you actually have a number of advantages with respect to what you can do compared with in-person groups. You can present virtually any type of stimuli, even go to a live website and click around in it while everyone observes in real time. It is also easy to obtain individual-level responses via numeric and short-answer polls or a public chat-box.

When using Adobe Connect's poll utility, I have found it best to go through my discussion guide and prepare in advance all of the polls I have planned. They can be stacked or placed to the side of the screen, outside of the group's view, and then dragged onscreen at the appropriate time. I introduce the poll and have group members complete it individually, almost always reading the question and answer categories to provide two channels of input and ensure that everyone is responding to the same stimulus.

As mentioned earlier, once all group members have answered, I usually click on the "broadcast" button, which shares a name-blinded summary of results with everyone, and also another button that shows me (but not the group members) who "voted" how. I then say something about the pattern of responses and facilitate a discussion about it. When appropriate, I name names to prod discussion, typically starting with a minority opinion. "Karen and Bill, you indicated that you really dislike the concept, tell me about it..." I then use their responses as a springboard for group discussion. This is an example of how it is easier with this kind of online group platform than it would be in-person to get "uncontaminated" individual responses and use them to prompt discussion.

I also mentioned that a back-room chat box has allowed me to communicate with the project team in real time (or as close to that as the platform allows – you have to be patient as there is always some lag between what is keyboarded and what you see onscreen) and either work out a new line of probing or restructure some or all of the remaining session depending on what we are hearing and seeing. For example, when I was exploring a new online tool for tracking one's energy use by appliance for a major electric utility, when group members uniformly panned both of the alternatives we were testing, the team and I redirected the remainder of the session away from comparative evaluation and toward what changes would satisfy participants.

Another possibility opened up by using an online platform to conduct a group comprised of participants from across different states, regions, or even countries is that it allows you to explore differences in local needs and conditions, as well as geographically based differences of opinion. With in-person groups, we commonly schedule sessions in different locations and then need to compare results after the fact. With online groups, you can bring out these differences and prompt discussion about them with individuals representing varying geographic segments, or segments with low prevalence in any one location, but which are represented by some group members from different areas. You can also bring together entire groups representing such thinly populated segments, low-incidence participant types (such as medical specialists treating a rare condition), by screening individuals from across geographic regions, something that simply may not be feasible even in a large metropolis like New York City, Los Angeles, Chicago, or Houston.

Downsides of online groups (and interviews)

There are currently three key downsides to using online depth research:

Unfamiliarity

One is that the technology puts off some clients who see it as novel, less trustworthy, having the potential to obtain different responses than in-person groups. (The same question has often been raised about online vs. telephone or in-person quantitative surveys.) This makes it all the more important to, first, assure potential users that virtual groups are a proven alternative and, then, if clients opt for online groups, ensure to the very best of your ability, that everything goes smoothly, with no operational glitches. For example, poor "show rates" for recruits, such as only two or three participants logging on to what was supposed to be an eight-person group, can lead clients to view the technology unfavorably and require you to reschedule the group. My general rule has been to do so if no more than three out of eight show for a full group but try to get the project team to accept four to five as an acceptable group size.

Team internet issues

Another problem occurs when the project team has not checked their own internet access to ensure that it is adequate. At Blackstone Group, we always send out an email to the project team and to clients asking them to test their connection for adequate bandwidth and then work with them if it fails. Once, my clients decided at the last moment to invite C-level executives and observe the group en masse from a conference room that proved to have a bad internet connection; all kind of problems occurred such as time lags and inability to see what was on the screen, and the team aborted the rest of the project. About all you can do in such a case is to prevent the problem by insisting that they test the connection in the same setting the project team will observe the groups in.

Moderator bandwidth

A third and, arguably, the most critical downside is that doing online groups take up more of the moderator's mental "bandwidth" than an in-person group. You have to pay attention to more different things all at once—all of the pods onscreen, what you are hearing, and participant's faces, which are harder to scan for expressions in video thumbnails than in-person, what's being keyboarded in the backroom chat, your discussion guide, thinking through your next thing to say or do. The first solution is practice, practice, and practice some more. With experience it gets a bit easier.

I have already referenced the most effective solution I know of, which the Blackstone Group has made a best practice: always have a second researcher assist in the role of tech support person. That person is the one to greet and help participants and project team members log on, get their webcams working properly, and then, during the group, handle any technical glitches, such as webcams or connections dropping out, which frequently happens, communicating privately with participants to solve any issues, and also to move polls and stimuli on and off the screen, and resize pods as needed. I would be very uncomfortable trying to do this all on my own and would probably end up with an unsatisfactory group experience for all. Experience makes it easier to deal with all these contingencies, while a dedicated tech support person enormously decreases the burden on the moderator and increases the probability of success.

CHAPTER 12

Depth Research Analysis

You've done depth research and that merits in-depth analysis. To really make sense out of what you have seen and heard, you need to step back and analyze the material systematically and dispassionately, which is what this section is all about.

Not all moderators are or want to be analysts

An appreciable proportion of professional moderators really do not like and have little or no interest in analysis and reporting. They are moderators, pure and simple. That's their job, as they see it, either by preference or by their role within a research unit, organization, or as independents. I have sometimes served as a hired moderator, and have also employed "pure" moderators to staff projects. It can be quite an appealing role. You show up, do some groups, hand everything off to other team members, pack up, go home, and collect your fee. There is something very seductive about flying around the country or the world doing just that, and, for some, very lucrative as well.

Still, it helps to understand what will be done with the material you generate, even if moderating is all you do. If you understand the analytic process, you can help to ensure the best possible outcome (and, hopefully, future work) by ensuring that you manage the group to generate the most useful and usable information. It comes down to the old Covey-esque saw, "begin with the end in mind."

For others, like me, moderating is an enjoyable and challenging skill, but at least as much joy comes from making practical sense of the information I obtain and communicating the results to clients or other stakeholders. Top-notch analysts are, it seems, less common than competent moderators. Although some research houses institutionalize a division of labor between moderators and analysts, overall there seems to be less demand for "pure" qualitative analysts than "pure" moderators. And I personally believe that even the most hands-off moderator should have some input into the analysis and at least be involved with reviewing and editing the final report to add their insights and ensure that it communicates accurately both the story and the feel of the groups.

Be that as it may, the payoff for any depth research project lies in the analysis. So let's talk about analyzing focus groups and depth interviews with an emphasis on the art and science of depth analysis, rather than on how to report or present qualitative findings. While there is necessarily some overlap, that topic merits a book in its own right.

The soul of qualitative analysis

The soul of qualitative analysis, as distinct from quantitative analysis, lies in its ability to tease out the "whys" behind what people do, think, feel, and say, how they relate to others and to things, and, ultimately, what "it's like" for them. While quantitative methods get at one level of the "how," in the sense of enabling us to isolate patterns out of the noise of events and behaviors, they do not really get at the "how" in the sense of "how people do things," how they actively construct their lives and the social realities within which they live those lives (Lofland, Snow, Anderson, and Lofland, 2005).

For example. I had just completed some qualitative research for the Executive Vice President of a supplier of medical and first aid supplies for schools, as the exploratory and foundational phase for a national survey. The goal of the project was to help them expand market share and penetration, especially among smaller school districts, to understand why they have lost some customer's business, and, literally, to get inside the heads of the school nurses who order supplies. After the qualitative phase, he remarked, "To sum it up, we positively have what we need now to form the questions in the Quantitative. I did not think we would get to the WHY — discounts, cheap/lower catalog prices, shipping, attending their regional conferences, limited school budgets and more supplies for their budgets were driving themes!"

The canons of logic and proof underlying qualitative methods are not based on statistical description or inference. Rather they follow what philosophers of science refer to as the "contextualist" or pragmatist approach (e.g., Pepper, 1970). The proper role of depth research is to provide actionable insights based on how things work, to figure out the story, the underlying patterns and processes and how they unfold or what they mean for the future, and how to get things done.

Another point is that you don't gather "data" from qualitative research, you get "material." (Blumer, 1965). This might seem to be a fussy distinction but semantics have impact. If you think of what you obtain from depth research as "data" you'll be tempted to focus on "objective facts." If you think of it as material, you're more likely to think of digging into that material to find out what's there, what you can learn from it, and what you can do with it. This goes back to the soul of qualitative analysis.

Casual vs. professional analysis

Time and again I've encountered the perception that qualitative analysis is easy, that it demands none of the rigor of quantitative analysis. It's something virtually anyone can do; you just look over your notes and report what happens and what it all means. See, it's not rocket science.

No, it's a different kind of science. Qualitative analysis falls within the great humanistic tradition that views human beings as actors, active subjects constructing their lives rather than passive objects who are acted upon by external and internal forces. We act, we strategize, we do things. This perspective is often seen as standing in opposition or contradiction to "science," but that is true only in the antiquated, mechanistic kind of science many of us were taught in school. That was before quantum physics, chaos theory, systems theory or even thermodynamics. Depth analysis, as I use the term here, is the application of systematic, professional qualitative analysis to depth research.

Depth analysis only looks simple

Bottom line: there is such a thing as rigorous, professional qualitative analysis. It digs beneath the surface of things, beyond appearances to understand how and why people do what they do and to understand the context within which (and which shapes how) we act and think as we do. Qualitative analysis is its own discipline. Truly professional qualitative analysis represents a blend of art and science; call it a craft, if you will. It is more than just "know-how," it is also "know what" and "know why" (and "why not"), with a little bit of "go by feel" attached—that's the art part.

One of the most frustrating issues with focus groups and depth interviews is how simple and straightforward it all seems from behind the mirror. Everyone thinks he or she is an expert. Clients often think "what you see is what you get," and that they have gotten it from watching and listening.

More than casual observation is required to get real value from depth research. A single focus group or interview is like a single data point. There is only so much information you can extract from it. In geometry, you need at least two points to draw a line, more to draw even the simplest shape. The same goes for depth research: to obtain anything like a systematic understanding, you need to conduct in-depth analysis across your entire study.

Depth analysis is more than just taking notes or getting discussion transcripts, reviewing them, thinking about it for a while, and writing up what you think the research has told you. The truly seasoned researcher/analyst may appear to do just that but it's like learning to play a musical instrument. First, you have to learn technique and practice, practice, practice. Eventually, as for any skilled craftsperson or performer, analysis may seem almost effortless, spontaneous, but to get beyond amateur status, you need a solid foundation of internalized technique coupled with experience and substantive knowledge. And you need to take a systematic approach.

Depth analysis gets at the "so what?"

While as I am fond of pointing out, the data cannot and does not "speak for itself," qualitatively derived material is even more innately mute. It just sits there until we wring meaning from it. That is the whole point of doing qualitative research—figuring out what it all means. The first step is determining what the patterns are, but the next and most crucial step for commercial and other applied research is making practical sense out of those patterns.

That is, answering the question, "So what?" Here's what you've learned — so figure out what it means, what's important about it, what needs to be done about it. "So what?" in that sense. Back to our parrot; this is the key to actionable analysis.

Mere description can be useful, but mainly for academic purposes. Marketing research (and applied social science research) is all about solving clients' or other sponsors' problems, gaining insight into issues, and generating actionable insights. As far as I am concerned, if it's not actionable, we have not done our job.

Avoiding analysis traps

On your way to the "so whats," the depth analyst needs to avoid any number of pitfalls.

Debriefing and the trap of on-the-spot analysis

We've all been asked to debrief after a session or two. As soon as you've finished your first evening of groups or a few interviews, clients and others in the back room may want to debrief you right then and there, on the spot. There's absolutely nothing wrong with that. In fact, a depth moderator needs to learn how to provide a factual debrief of what she or he perceives went on, what it means, and what implications that might have with respect to the research, the research objectives, and for the client. It goes a bit farther than "just the facts," but not much farther or else you're creating a monster.

Don't get caught in the trap of on-the-spot analysis.

How many times has a moderator popped into the back room only to discover that the client team wants a debrief after a session or two, and then goes ahead and makes the decisions the program of research was designed to inform? They might not even wait for you. Sometimes at least a few of them have packed up and left even before you go back there. At other times, a project team member shows up at a session part of the way through the research, gets a snap impression and runs with it. This can be particularly troublesome if that was a senior person, internal client, or other decision-maker.

What's wrong with making decisions based on this kind of quick, on-the-spot analysis? Nothing, insofar as it goes. It just does not go very far and certainly not far enough to act upon.

- **You're betting that a subset of events will be truly representative.** Who knows what will happen in the next event, or what kind of new things you will learn, what additional facts, or insights will emerge? Sometimes the next event or set of events may lead you to reframe your thinking, or will stand in direct contradiction to the last one. You never know, and you can never know. We are back to the issue of a single data point.
- **There is a natural tendency to pick out what impresses you.** Objective analysis requires you to stand back from the event and to look at it impassively. We all tend to notice, recall, and respond to the most interesting, memorable, provocative, strongly put, or otherwise literally outstanding statements or events that occurred. Similarly, we remember the strongest, most interesting, provocative, or most authoritative person, and the ones who most strongly voice their opinions. The problem is that this can overshadow our memory or otherwise mask other voices, other viewpoints or statements. At best, it's only part of the picture. At worst, it can be terribly misleading. We tend to remember the first and last things said and focus on statements we agree or disagree with strongly.
- **There is also the problem of selective focus.** The psychology of

memory and attention teaches us that people tend to focus on only a part of the whole. You cannot pay equal attention to everything at once or even at a particular moment, let alone over the course of an hour or two of focus group activity. More than that, our minds work by telling ourselves stories to make sense out of what we see, hear and feel; if something does not fit into the story we are constructing, we tend to push it off somewhere into the background.

Observer bias

These problems are compounded by the reality that, in any research, there are no completely objective observers. In fact, those behind the mirror are commonly embroiled in various professional/political struggles and are liable to interpret what goes on in that light. We tend to notice and recall things that we are expecting (or that radically depart from our expectations), things we are personally interested in, and, often, on things that confirm our going-in beliefs, assumptions, needs, and perspectives. We all bring ourselves, with all our personal biases, assumptions, and presumptions to observation. Psychologically, we tend to use that as an organizing principle.

Sometimes there is a blatant, explicit controversy going on, which the research may be at least in part intended to help resolve. Other times, it is a matter of our product versus theirs, so that marketers will focus on anything or everything that supports their "baby" and its value. One often hears some variation of "See, I told you . . ." after a group. That's not a product of sound analysis, even if it is 100 percent correct! The same is true far outside of the marketing research context, even in formal experimental research as another of my mentors, Theodore X. Barber, pointed out in his incisive book, *Pitfalls in Human Research* (2013).

Moderator bias

There is also moderator bias. The moderator may not be the best person to give an objective analysis of what just went on in a group or interview, at least not before some time has passed. Rather, just like behind-the-mirror observers, we tend to be impressed by certain statements, participants, exchanges, or the like. I, for example, routinely generate working hypotheses as I conduct a session to guide my moderating, but which may or may not prove to be valid on careful scrutiny or after I have, literally, had a chance to sleep on it. We may find that we like (and start to root for) a particular participant, concept, idea, product or option and dislike others. This can bias our memory of what transpired. Experienced moderators try as hard as they can to be as objective as possible, but we are human beings and subject to human limitations.

Even ignoring the possibility of such bias, it is a bad bet to assume that we walk away from the group with a clear, encyclopedic memory of what went on. Sometimes we do, but, as I've pointed out, the moderator's attention is at best, split during the session, even more so when we're doing online focus groups. Not everything that transpires will register fully and accurately in our minds. Focus group participants may, for example, speak over one another, or you may not hear or notice what everyone says. For one thing, that's why I like to get transcripts.

Slow down, don't move too fast

These are all reasons why it is essential to conduct a dispassionate, objective, and systematic analysis before we generate formal conclusions and recommendations to our clients. This is also important to make clear to our clients and end users of the research. We need to educate them, as best we can, to allow us to complete and systematically analyze the research.

Marketers, salespeople and anyone else involved in a project as clients or potential users of the findings often want to run with their impressions before it is all over, the more senior generally the more so (and with less tolerance for waiting until all the evidence is in and analyzed before acting). On the spot analysis can lead to useful working hypotheses, but little else.

Part of the moderator's job is to keep observers from literally jumping to conclusions because they are liable to jump the wrong way, sometimes the equivalent of leaping off a cliff they didn't realize was there, with others in the back room following like lemmings. As I've mentioned, sometimes you end your session and go into the backroom to discover that key decision makers have already packed up and left. Sometimes they do not continue to attend the rest of the scheduled sessions. This becomes even more problematic when team members and their internal clients are observing remotely, via videostreaming or video conferencing or watching a video of the session at a later time, so that we have no chance to intervene in what might be termed "premature conclusion."

It takes time and effort to reach satisfying, sound conclusions. It takes discipline and systematic effort. While inspiration has its place, making practical sense out of focus groups takes time and work.

Styles of depth research analysis

Now it's time to get pragmatic and consider what this "work" involves. Over the years, I have encountered two basic styles of depth analysis.

Reportage

The first and most basic of these might be termed "reportage." Reliance on this mode is typical of apprentice-level qualitative analysts, but even the most seasoned master will employ it when and where appropriate. It boils down to describing or presenting what went on during the group.

The naïve moderator, client, or other observer may assume that all one needs to do is to listen to and watch a group or interview, take some notes, perhaps compare it with what one recalls from previous events, write up a top line summary, and that's the analysis. Unfortunately, this approach give you merely a surface impression of what transpired.

Top line reports

The most commonly used type of reportage is the top line or "executive top line" report. Clients usually expect some kind of top line summary after each focus group or set of focus groups within a day or two of completion. A top line or executive summary is commonly requested or offered as part of the research proposal. To offer real value, even a top line needs to be thought through carefully and objectively.

The pure top line is a bullet-point summary of what transpired during the group or set of groups. There is little or no depth of analysis, few if any quotes and, typically, only a précis of the methodology, sample, timing, and place of events. This can be deliberate, recognizing that no systematic analysis has been done, or it might reflect naïveté, lack of understanding what qualitative analysis can and should be. In many instances, the more seasoned practitioner will include at least some key findings or conclusions, based on her or his shorthand analysis of what transpired. Ideally, the report at this stage is ringed with caveats cautioning readers that the findings are provisional.

There is another type of reportage sometimes presented as a final deliverable, the verbatim-based report. The "analyst" (I put that in ironic quotes deliberately) assembles direct quotations from the transcript or notes, perhaps grouping them by subject or within the framework of the discussion guide's sequence of topics and questions. Verbatim quotes (the term "verbatim" meaning a literal, word-for-word direct quotation) are treated as data and allowed to speak for themselves. In such a report, there may be a section on methodology, sample, time, and place of events, perhaps some summary of key findings, but the verbatim information is being used to tell the story of what transpired and to present what was learned.

Formally trained qualitative methodologists like myself are likely to find this approach deeply lacking, amateurish, and unprofessional, in a class with quantitative tab-and-field reports that present table after table of data without any real integration or interpretation. Moreover, the data tables at least present the full range of responses in their actual frequencies; compiled verbatims ultimately reflect the analyst's subjective choices of what to pick out from an hour or two of discussion. This leaves lots of room for bias, whether witting or unwitting, and can misrepresent what actually went on, for example, by giving "equal time" to positive and negative comments.

Some practitioners would likely disagree, finding this approach to be perfectly acceptable. No accounting for tastes, and all that. In my opinion, a verbatim-based report is not an adequate final deliverable, but can be valuable "top" or "first-level" analysis, as it is sometimes called. For example, it may be useful when deploying multiple moderators to have them provide summary reports to a lead analyst, who is responsible for in-depth analysis.

Hopefully, the verbatim statements will be rationally organized (if only by where they fit within the discussion guide or focus group outline) and interspersed with some interpretative or reflective commentary.

Systematic depth analysis

Reportage stands in contrast to what I term "systematic depth analysis." There is a formal process involved, which teases out the patterns to be found in the qualitative material. Applied researchers and analysts do not stop at identifying or describing those patterns. Rather, they work "with the end in mind," recognizing that this is not an academic enterprise but, rather, research designed to guide, support, or evaluate real-world actions, or decisions. As I've suggested above, we focus on the "so what," not just on the "what." This is a keynote of the approach.

Although individual analysts and research suppliers may have their own variations, there are two basic approaches to the systematic qualitative analysis of depth research:

Naturalistic analysis

Although most depth research moderators and analysts do not realize it, the methodology generally used to analyze focus groups, like the very concept of a "focus group," stems from the sociological social science tradition. The overall idea is to review notes or transcripts, compare all instances of discussion relating to a particular topic or question and then summarize themes and variations. Commonly, the depth research analyst goes through the discussion guide to identify categories for comparison in this manner. You might also go directly to the questions or topics relevant to the study objectives, or even the client's request for proposal, and use these as the categories.

While anthropologists doing ethnography and earlier qualitative sociologists employed and described similar methods, the basic approach I am presenting here was codified by Barney Glaser and Anselm Strauss in their 1967 manifesto, *The Discovery of Grounded Theory* (in which the term "discovery" is used as an active verb). They argued that the qualitative analyst should not start with hypotheses or assume you know virtually anything about what you will find, but should build one's understanding literally with a ground-up approach. Let the material tell you what's going on, in other words. In the authors' opinion, this is a guiding canon of professional qualitative analysis. This approach has been extended and further defined by a newer generation of grounded theorists, like Kathy Charmez (2014), but here we'll stick to the basics.

Glaser and Strauss termed their basic analytic technique the constant comparative method. Oversimplifying a bit, you take "field notes" capturing what you observe. The equivalent in most depth research today is having sessions transcribed, typically in Microsoft Word or Excel. You then go through these notes in a systematic way, comparing and contrasting what you see to identify threads or what grounded theorists term "basic social processes." You build a theoretical map of these processes and that's your analysis. Since then, Glaser and Strauss each evolved their own variant forms of grounded theory, but these are the basics.

Content analysis

Content analysis (and variations like sentiment analysis), is another approach sometimes used with depth research. It boils down to formally studying the contents of the communications by and among study participants including any "text" or other communications artifacts such as photos or videos. This may involve identifying the words or phrases used by participants or appearing in the transcripts, the relationships among these terms, and the like. While quite a few researchers and analysts use this term very loosely, to describe identifying terms used by research subjects and the implications of how and when they are used, there is a whole range of methodologies and techniques to which this label is applied, differing among academic disciplines, commercial providers, as well as individual practitioners. A formal content analysis boils down to counting, coding, reporting, and analyzing frequencies and relationships among terms and, today, is generally done with computer programs, increasingly employing machine learning, which makes it seem very "scientific" or "high tech," and therefore impressive.

While I have done some informal content analysis in the process of analyzing depth research, formal content analysis is a specialized technique that can be very useful in at least some circumstances. I have yet to find a situation where it seems appropriate but there are numerous texts available for the depth researcher wishing to learn more about this approach (e.g., Krippendorff, 2004).

Word clouds are an increasingly popular tweak on content analysis that marketers and researchers tend to like and which I have found useful as part of depth analysis where appropriate. Basically, word clouds provide a graphical representation of the frequency with which specific words or phrases are used in a particular text (which can be an excerpt from a transcript or an entire transcript). Most readers have seen and possibly used word clouds themselves. There are also variations, such as "word trees," that visually show the connection of words in the text or dataset, providing some context. In addition to firms and analysts who specialize in developing these types of content analyses for clients, you can find a number of free programs on the web. Here, for example is a word cloud derived from Chapter One of this book using the free program available at *https://wordart.com/:*

CHAPTER 13

Doing Depth Research Analysis

Now, let's turn to the practical issue of how to go about doing depth research analysis following the canons of qualitative social science methodology.

Raw material

Obviously, one needs raw material on which to conduct the analysis. Below are the most widely used ways of obtaining this, in order of increasing relative cost.

Memory

Your memory is necessary but not sufficient as the basis for analysis. As a moderator, I rely on my memory to keep the big picture in mind and to help me keep other records of what transpired in context, to flag what's missing or not quite right as I proceed with my analysis, and to fill in any blanks I find as I do so. However, even the best, freshest, and most acute memory is not a sound basis for analysis. Of course, a moderator pretty much has to rely on their memory for immediate, post-session briefings or memos. It may be all you have to work from for a quick-turnaround top line, But relying on memory alone, as suggested earlier, is incompatible with systematic analysis.

Memory is simply not trustworthy enough to serve as the basis for important decision or follow-up actions, just as witness reports have been shown to be problematic in legal proceedings. In the metaphor of General Semantics, memory is neither the true map of the territory nor a map of all the territory. All memory is from the individual's perspective. In fact, the study of people's accounts regrading "what actually happened" is the subject of "ethnomethodology," an entire field of social psychology (Garfinkle, 1967). Furthermore, memory dissipates.

Moderator's notes

Your own notes are likely to be a less subjective and more permanent way to capture what has gone on in your depth research than memory alone. But it's hard—heck, virtually impossible—to capture everything in your notes while engaged in moderating, harder to do so without bias, without distracting yourself by splitting attention, and even harder to do so in a way that you can decipher later!

Nevertheless, memory and moderator's notes are required to answer on-the-spot questions. I commonly take minimal notes during in-person groups and interviews. This helps me to keep my focus on the information being exchanged and serves to capture key topics or responses as an aid to questioning as well as a reminder of things to check or include in analysis. When doing online groups, in particular, I have come to take fewer, if any notes, in order to allow myself to focus better on managing the discussion, onscreen polls or graphics, and back-room chat.

One major challenge is learning how to take notes that you can decipher later. Qualitative researchers like the author's colleague Brian Sherman may train themselves to take notes without looking down (Sherman and Straus, 2002). A truly excellent touch typist could keyboard notes at the same time they are moderating although any typing sounds might be distracting, online especially. I find it easier to scrawl down some notes, maybe a page, at most two, for an entire group. When the project does not allow for transcriptions and time is short, a seasoned moderator can, in fact, use such notes as the basis for top lines and, if necessary, informal analysis and reporting, but to do so effectively requires a great deal of experience, a sharp memory, and substantive knowledge.

I may be contradicting myself, but when doing a lot of depth interviews, particularly—but not only—when there are multiple interviewers, I do commonly rely on notes. I take the discussion guide and convert it into a note-taking guide, adding a place for the date and time, interviewee's name and other key information (like segment) in the upper header section, then creating white space below topics or groups of questions to enter notes. I usually minimize margins and expand font size, then put the form together with a diagonal staple allowing pages to be turned easily.

Observers' notes

Having a note-taker can be an excellent alternative. In my first marketing research job, I spent over a year in the back room, taking notes and then analyzing them. This was superb training in observing a master like Al Goldman doing groups and then learning to analyze them. I strongly recommend this practice as a training method for new moderators, or when moderators do groups in subject areas with which they are unfamiliar.

However, in this day of increasingly restricted budgets and pricing, even large commercial marketing research projects generally cannot afford to have an individual attend depth research solely as note-taker. Clients often like having that second person in the back room, whether or not they serve as note-taker, but someone has to cover their time and, typically travel. Note-takers can also help manage the backroom while you're moderating. This may be easier to bring off in non-commercial, academic, or other applied settings and well-funded projects where one can assign note-taking responsibility to interns or other team members whose compensation is not a budgetary issue.

Audio and/or video recordings

Recordings are the best, most practical way to ensure that you get it right. The analyst can work directly from sound or video recordings of the group. You can, of course, take notes from these sources and use them as field notes for analysis.

However, this can be very time-consuming, requiring you to shuttle back and forth several times from the recording to your notes, but it may be a good, practical option when the analyst does not have access to full transcripts. And, of course, audio or video files are used as the raw materials for transcription. In addition to providing the inputs for that, recordings let you go back and find quotes, clarify transcribed material, or check to make sure that your analysis covers all bases. Visual recordings further enable you to observe or check non-verbal behaviors, even body language, at least to some degree and, if there will be need to use multimedia recordings for such purposes, you might consider upgrading recordings of in-person sessions to hiring a videographer with professional-grade equipment and documentary skills, or upgrading online video-capture technology when possible.

Recording, audio or visual, can be edited, with excerpts used in reports and presentations, or as input into analytic software programs. You can conduct specialized analyses from video transcripts, such as formal interactional analysis, conversational analysis, or the like, although this adds cost and complexity and is not widely used, at least in marketing research. The bottom line is that, if nothing else, recordings provide a permanent record of the event, although privacy regulations and legalistic concerns may require editing out personally identifiable content (even pixilating faces), or restrict the length of time for which the recordings are retained.

Transcripts

Transcriptions of the recorded session are currently the optimal source for depth analysis today, in my opinion and experience. They are preferably done in a text-based program, like Word or Pages, or in a spreadsheet like Excel. Such software allows you to work with the transcripts easily and conveniently. Avoid having transcripts saved as pdf files or other formats that you cannot easily cut and paste or otherwise modify.

Until recently, you needed to manually transcribe sessions from audio or video recordings. Hiring out transcription can be expensive and turnaround can be slow. A few leading edge firms are offering fully automated but reportedly rough transcriptions, with other suppliers like Rev.com using artificial intelligence in combination with freelancers to provide low-cost, quick-turnaround transcription.

Pending full automation, it is a good practice to provide the transcriptionist with some background, such as discussion guides and lists of terms or brand names used in the sessions that may be unfamiliar to that individual. This is particularly important when doing highly technical research dealing with medical/healthcare, technology, or specialized business topics. The primary issue with transcripts is that they require some additional time before analysis and can add appreciably to project costs.

Transcription services vary in how they present focus group data. The most useful text-based transcripts look rather like scripts for a play, identifying speakers individually (if only as Number 1, Number 2, and so forth). It is best if transcripts cut out "hems and haws," sidebar conversations not germane to the group, or other bits (like partial phrases followed by a full statement) that do not directly contribute to analysis. There are also newer technologies and variations that can extend the value and usability of transcripts.

Self-explicated material

Self-explicated individual-level responses provided by participants through written or online polls, short-answer questions, and chat boxes provide an extremely valuable supplement to group discussion and can facilitate analysis of depth interviews, as well. Online platforms can, as noted earlier, allow you to have group members provide individual-level information or responses through a chat box. Additionally, you can get individuals' responses to, interpretation of, or associations with graphical or visual stimuli using whiteboard or other technology, such as virtual post-it notes.

■ Sources of Material for Depth Analysis

Source	Pluses	Minuses
Memory	Immediate access; can capture all aspects of interactions; no added time or cost	Selective attention, recall and bias issues; impermanence – rapid fading of memory
Moderator's Notes	Immediate access; no additional personnel, time or cost needed; permanent record; can capture nonverbal elements	Hard to take full, readable notes while moderating; can be distracting; splits focus, reducing moderator effectiveness and information capture; selective attention, recall and bias issues

Source	Pluses	Minuses
Observer's Notes	Can be objective and comprehensive; permanent record; can be done on computer; can capture non-verbal aspects	Need experienced note-taker; may not capture everything (e.g., differing reactions, things going on in a corner); can add cost
Audio Recordings	Capture all verbal interaction objectively; permanent record; automatic transcription now available; can be used in deliverables	Only capture spoken material, missing nonverbals; transcription adds cost; may be suboptimal without good transcriptionist
Video Recordings	Go beyond audio to capture visual content, non-verbal responses; can help in deciphering verbal statements; operator-assisted option allows highest quality, complete record; allow visual analysis; can be used in deliverables	Same as audio; add cost; depend on ability of camera, set-up to capture everything important or potentially meaningful; operators expensive; may require special equipment, software, training to analyze visual elements formally
Transcripts	Capture all verbal content objectively; provide permanent, easily accessed record; facilitate analysis; can be done on computer; automated transcripts now available; can use as input to text analysis software (e.g., word cloud generators)	To capture all aspects accurately and completely, need well-trained transcriptionist; "inaudibility" glitches frequent; issues with homonyms, technical terminology; add significant cost; do not typically capture visual information
Self-Explicated Inputs: Polls, Quizzes, Chats, Whiteboard Overlay, Other Tools	Facilitate individual-level data collection; supplement discussion with other inputs potentially including survey-like numbers, short-answer responses; can use various supplementary tools for markup, etc.; can be treated like data if sample size adequate	Need to be collected and collated; do not typically meet norms for statistical data collection and sampling; can be misleading/spurious or easily mistaken for statistically valid, reliable data and misused (especially if very small samples)

Naturalistic analysis

Perhaps the most useful codification of how to do "naturalistic" analysis is an out-of-print classic by Anselm Strauss and his student/colleague Leonard Schatzman (1973). A second, still-available classic on the topic, now in its fourth edition, is *Analyzing Social Settings,* (Lofland, Snow, Anderson and Lofland, 2005), which provides countless useful tips on naturalistic analysis, coming from a slightly different angle than Schatzman and Strauss. I was trained in these "naturalistic" approaches by one of the book's senior authors, John Lofland as a doctoral student specializing in qualitative methodology and that continues to frame and inspire how I personally conduct depth analysis. The central concept is to pour over one's "field notes" (which can also take the form of a transcript), "code" them for key analytic elements, aggregate all the cases of the same code, perhaps develop sub-codes, and then use a "compare and contrast" approach enabling you to draw out the underlying "concepts."

Coding and Stacking: Doing Naturalistic Analysis the Original Way

To explain the basic process of naturalistic analysis, let's go back a few decades to a time when we had to rely on copy machines or, even earlier, carbon copies and review the original approach to doing naturalistic analysis. Here are the basic steps that would apply to analyzing depth research material:

1. **Transcribe all the events** (field notes). There may be pages and pages of notes, commonly one bunch or pile per interview or group.
2. **Read through your notes to get an overall sense of what's there.** It's best to go through all examples of each respondent segment or type, and then go to the next type, and so on. Use your discussion guide as your outline to identify the questions and topics to look for.
3. **Now, grab your first bunch of notes and do what grounded theorists call "theoretical coding."** Take a highlighter (you'll want to use different colors for different topics or other groupings) or draw brackets in the margin to indicate segments of the notes that relate to different topics, parts of the story, or types of questions or responses. Label each of these (that is, code them) and keep a record of your labels.
4. **Make copies of each coded set of notes, lots of copies.** (Remember we are talking about the "olden days," before everyone had a PC or Mac)
5. **Go to the first copy and, literally, cut it up into strips by code segment.** You will typically identify more than one occurrence of

each code in a single transcript or event. These can (and often do) overlap, so a particular exchange or statement may be partially or completely associated with several different codes. Just cut out all those snippets pertaining to a single code. That's one reason why you make up a lot of copies. There will also be parts that do not fit any segment and will be discarded.

6. **Now, start making stacks.** Put each set of paper strips for a single code into its own stack.
7. **Go to your next copy set and cut it up to create strips for any codes that overlapped other codes.** Sort them into stacks, whether stacks you have already started or new ones. Repeat until done cutting strips for all code segments you have marked.
8. **Grab a stack. Read all the strips in it.** If any don't belong, put them into a stack where they belong.
9. **Take this "coding" process a level or two deeper, breaking down the stack into subsets that represent similar parts of the story.** Again, it's a matter of comparing the material on your paper strips (hence "the constant comparative method"), possibly annotating them with new codes, and then sorting them into smaller stacks or grabbing another copy of the notes and slicing it up to do so. Keep going through that stack until it's done and you are assured that it all fits together and that you have broken out all relevant sub-groupings. I would sometimes pile up these sub-stacks at right angles to each other while keeping them in the same vertical stack.
10. **Repeat for all stacks.** Continue sorting, subdividing, and re-sorting your material until you are satisfied you have broken the story down into its key units.
11. **Now start processing your stacks,** letting the story emerge from the material itself. Read each of the strips in each stack and/or sub-stack, figure out what the unifying theme is, compare and contrast instances on that theme. Check if your codes really fit, otherwise rename the themes or groupings. Move them around,

reordering them as appropriate. Decide which, if any, quotes to keep as "verbatims" (see below). Restack the material vertically in order or in whatever manner you want to organize each stack.

12. **Put the stacks into a logical sequence.** Essentially, each stack is a chapter or other molecular element of your story. The next step is to put them into a meaningful sequence, outlining your narrative, so to speak. Doing it by hand with paper strips, if you had the room, you'd put the stacks into linear sequences, say working from left to right, trying out first one then another sequence until the flow "clicked" for you.
13. **Now assemble them. We used to do this by Scotch taping, pasting or gluing the pieces together.** This is the original "cut and paste."

Viola! That's your basic analysis. Go through it and write the body of your report. This legacy method was wonderfully tactile. Like a book vs. an electronic reader, it also had the advantage of having all the "pages" out there in the physical world, so you could pick them up and read them, dog ear them, scrawl notes on the margin.

However, the mechanical process was very labor intensive and time consuming. Cumbersome is an understatement, and it required a lot of space. John Lofland, who taught me this method at U.C. Davis, converted his garage into a study and installed shelves around three walls so he would have enough room for all his code-stacks.

Computer-Assisted method

Today, your PC or Mac computer can take over many of the mechanical steps described above. Nevertheless, what we do boils down to the same process, which is why it is important to understand this "legacy" approach. The simplest way in which today's analyst can use digital technology to facilitate depth analysis might be termed the *computer-assisted method.* You use standard word processing software to eliminate much of the more cumbersome aspects of that original by-hand method, with a lot less time and effort. You "drag and drop" rather than "cut and paste." But the basic process is still the same, making virtual rather than physical stacks, sorting, comparing, moving them around, and letting the story emerge. Here's a simplified description of how I might go about doing computer-assisted analysis today:

1. **Create a master file** to paste your material in a logical sequence. I typically start, at least, by creating sections based on the discussion guide, in the same sequence as they appear. You can always change, subdivide, or reorder them later, understanding that nothing is sacrosanct, everything is subject to revision, and reordering as the analysis evolves; this is still the constant comparative method. Now put the file aside for the moment. I typically use Microsoft Word for this although some might prefer Excel.
2. **Read through each transcript or section of notes and highlight material** or use different font colors to capture sections and to indicate which are important, which verbatim may be a "keeper," and perhaps annotate it. You can, of course, just do that in your mind.
3. **Go back through your first transcript, and cut and paste into your master file from it.** Be sure to keep the originals intact and work with copies. Otherwise, you can end up with a mess of partial bits and pieces that make no sense.
4. **Make use of the Word and similar programs' ability to open multiple windows. I'd suggest, if possible, making at least two windows visible at once by reducing** their size to part-screen. For example, keep your master file onscreen and then open a note file or transcript. Now you can easily drag and drop material from that into your master file.
5. **Go through each transcript, drag and drop any relevant material into the appropriate sections of your master file.** You are creating virtual analogs of the original stacks and sub-stacks. Generally, I have several parts of a discussion guide section on each page, which I typically demarcate by typing in sub-section headers all in caps.
   - **Do it with quotes.** While I may enter some "notes" as such, I find it expedient to lift quotes from the actual transcript, as

necessary combining sequential bits and pieces that convey what participants are saying (for example, skipping over or sometimes including the moderator's probes that come between parts of a complete thought or statement). This saves time later and also provides more context than a note regarding what is being said. If you do this, be sure to code them in some way so that you can attribute them or, at least, know who said them and what their segment was.

– **Lists and informal counts.** For topics where I will want to create counts or lists of variations, I normally enter a header and then create a list below that, possibly starting with a few options that I know or expect to find, using an "x" as a tick mark. For example, when I come across the first case of an item I want to include in such a list, I type in the word or name and put an "x" to the right of it (as that's the first instance), then another x for the second occasion. I may also paste in some relevant quotes under the category and before the next category. In this way, you can assemble your story — that is, your analysis — onscreen. Just drag and drop.

6. **Enter any notes as you go.** As you think of them (or they emerge), you can note both conclusions and implications and front-end material such as methodological points, sample or group timing, and composition information. You might, for example, use Word's "comments" tool for your notes. Alternatively, I like to enter comments in all caps and then highlight the note for easy finding later.
7. **Don't worry about details as you do this analysis.** Spelling does not count, nor does grammar, until you prepare the final product.
8. **Process as you go according to the constant comparative method;** keep comparing, contrasting, teasing out concepts, and story line. Reorder, subdivide, sequence, test the logic, and flow. Then do it again, and again, until the whole story comes to life. Remember the basic strategy of grounded and naturalistic qualitative analysis: let

the story emerge from the material. You should by all means generate working hypotheses to guide your thinking, but keep checking against the material and let your hypotheses change and evolve.

9. **Before you're done, be sure to go back and check the proposal,** to ensure that you are covering all the bases as promised and meeting the study objectives. Also, go back to the discussion guide to ensure that you've covered everything.

With lots of experience, you will find that you can do much of the organization and compare-and-contrast in your head and you can do it much faster. That's good for rapid turnaround situations, but it will continue to pay off to externalize the work. Get it out of your mind, onto a computer screen at least and use a systematic method.

Computerized analysis

Another way to accomplish the same basic tasks is fully computerized analysis. You employ specialized software that can provide more sophisticated manipulation of the qualitative material. While the highest level of this can be almost completely automated (and may eventually involve AI programs that replace the analyst), down to grouping and analyzing the material. At that extreme it becomes essentially indistinguishable from a quantitative analysis. For example, my late friend, Dr. Charles Cleveland, a clinical sociologist and founder of CDC Questor, developed software and procedures to analyze short verbal transcripts that his firm has used for several decades. He first applied this technology in the original study of interest-bearing checking accounts back in the 1970s and claimed he used it to develop the slogan of pork "as the other white meat."

More commonly, analysts may use specialized software programs to assist in qualitative analysis. Ethnograph is the only one that I have actually used but you can find any number of programs for qualitative analysis online. However, such programs are not easy to learn or master. You might want to consider taking a course to learn how to use them. Personally, I've never found it worth the time, cost, and hassle to use any of these programs, although they might offer significant value in processing truly huge, multi-moderator projects where there is an overwhelming amount of material to code and analyze.

Verbatim quotes

Qualitative reports typically include selected verbatim statements (quotations) but are they evidence, support, or illustration? This is actually a profound and deeply meaningful question with which the depth analyst must grapple. Although we are obviously going into reporting, despite my promise not to do so, this is something the depth analyst must take into consideration. And, as mentioned earlier, I often build my analytic notes by dragging and dropping relevant verbatims from transcripts. Then, in the report writing phase, I can go back and find appropriate verbatims to enhance reportage.

The consensus among social science methodologists is that the heart of qualitative analysis should be the concepts, generalizations, and story elements one derives. Verbatims should be used, in moderation, to illustrate key points and perspectives; to communicate the qualities or flavor of the focus group discussion. They can bring the results to life, literally let your audience get the qualitative feel for what transpired, what the group's interactions were like, something that is almost impossible to convey in rational, formal analytic terms or prose.

How verbatim?

Do you have to present quotations literally verbatim, that is, as something you might cut and paste directly from a transcript, "ums" and parenthetical comments and all? While this is somewhat controversial in marketing research circles, qualitative sociologists (like Lofland and myself) contend it is perfectly acceptable to omit such rhetorical stutters, to use ellipses (. . .) to bridge over irrelevant bits, or even to occasionally paraphrase in order to bring out the central thought. Why? We use verbatim material to illustrate points not as evidence or in place of higher-level analysis. Those with a more journalistic bent may prefer to lift the quote in its entirety from the recording or transcript. However, most seasoned focus group analysts tend to follow the social scientist's approach.

In summary, then, the proper use of verbatims in depth research reports is primarily for purposes of illustration, to bring the audience "inside" the subjective (qualitative) feeling of group interactions, and secondarily to lend support to discursive commentary regarding concepts or findings. Verbatims, however, should not be treated as "data" or, in that sense, as "evidence," although you can certainly use them when building your analytic notes.

Role of numbers in depth analysis

As I've noted earlier, when doing depth research, you cannot easily or always get away from those pesky numbers. Clients want numbers—rankings, ratings, counts. Many researchers obtain numbers almost reflexively, without really considering the methodological implications. There are valid ways of incorporating and using numbers in purely qualitative and quantitatively enhanced depth research. Polls, rankings, ratings, counts all can provide extremely useful insights and can be useful in their own right, as long as that numeric material is used appropriately.

What is "appropriately?" Used in the strictest qualitative manner, numeric material is fodder or stimuli for discussion and probing while moderating. "Two of you said this, and five said that, tell me about it . . ." But remember that the "soul" of qualitative analysis lies in understanding the whys, not the whats or how many. Those are the proper domain of quantitative research.

"Qualitative" numbers have their uses, nevertheless. For instance, as rough, directional indicators of opinions, realities on the ground, or behavior. Reporting on the numbers from focus groups or interviews can be a useful shorthand, and does provide some limited insight; sometimes those are the only numbers your clients will have. However, as the author likes to tell more "numerate" clients and focus group members (such as doctors, scientists, or engineers), when we ask them for numbers, percentages, or counts: due to the small sample size of a single group, the confidence interval is as wide as the state in which the research event is being held, so we're not going to use those numbers for purposes of statistical analysis.

For individual groups or fewer than about ten interviews, my preferred approach in most cases is to reference and report the actual numbers, not percentages or means. "Four out of five group participants said or felt thus and such," is a powerful statement and suggests a lot of implications, but is less misleading than saying "80 percent of group members . . ." Some well-informed research-trained clients make it clear that they do not want any numbers reported, knowing that their internal clients and even peers are likely to assume that these numbers are statistically reliable and valid and use them to make decisions. But these seem to be a small minority among clients.

On the other hand, as mentioned earlier, if your sample sizes overall or for any participant segment get up to 30 or more, you can do some legitimate basic statistics on that — so long as you make it clear that the "data" does not conform to key norms of quantitative research with respect to sampling. Also, when you do a formal survey everything is controlled to avoid changing the context of questioning so as to introduce bias. Even when an interviewer administers a telephone survey, the same questions are asked in the same sequence (except for skip patterns, or randomization), without any interpretation (beyond "whatever that means to you"). Polls and other numeric exercises in a focus group context, in contrast, are done amidst discussions so that the context of response is different in every group. So keep those caveats in mind!

Keep in mind also how very easy and tempting it can be to misuse the numbers generated in focus groups. I and like-minded qualitative methodologists are very dubious about the widespread practice of reporting means or other statistics for the numbers collected in a few sessions or (we shudder to think of it) a single focus group or interview. We believe this is terribly likely to mislead our clients and give the impression of false accuracy or "statistical" findings. Numbers that small are not statistically stable or meaningful. Clients would be ill advised to "run" with such numbers in marketing or use them to make business decisions. It is the qualitative researcher's obligation, we feel, to advise them against that and to present numeric information in a way that reduces the likelihood of over-interpretation and misuse.

Drawing conclusions, insights and actionable recommendations

I was startled recently, when responding to an RFP (Request for Proposal) from a major health insurance company, where one of the questions was "Describe your organization's experience in building an actionable report that not only describes main findings but also provides business insights." My response was, "As far as we are concerned, there is no other type of report!"

If the report does not provide actionable business insights, the marketing research firm has failed to provide full value. The same is true for virtually any other applied research situation. If it's not actionable, it's not right. Think in terms of four levels of depth research analytics:

■ Four Levels of Depth Research Analysis

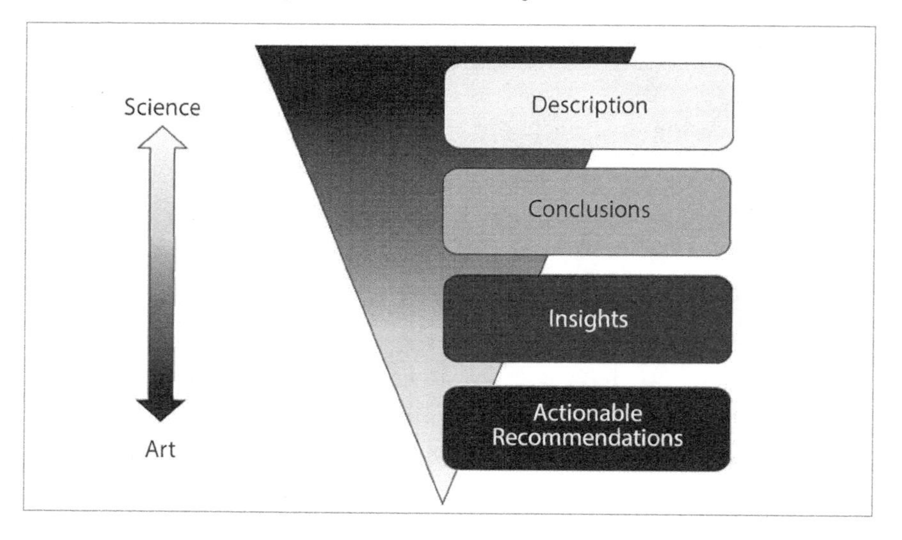

Description

Description is the most "objective" and mechanistic level of depth research analysis. It involves simply teasing out (and ultimately, reporting) what is there, in your transcripts or recordings. Doing it well requires you, at least, to create some kind of structure within which to sort and organize observations in order for the analysis to be at all meaningful and useful.

While the easiest level of qualitative analytics to accomplish, requiring the least skill or substantive knowledge, it is also generally the most appropriate level at which to develop top line reports: "the facts, nothing but the facts." Outside of that context, going no further than descriptive analysis offers the least client value of the four levels and is generally avoided by professional researchers or analysts. We would consider this, essentially, to be the raw material from which to proceed.

Conclusions

Drawing and presenting conclusions requires some degree of artfulness in teasing out meaningful generalizations from your material. You need to sort through all the possible generalizations that can be drawn from the patterns observed in (to adapt a phrase from the great psychologist, William James) the big, blooming buzzing confusion of your material. This, one might say, is the level of drawing out what we learned from all those facts.

Drawing conclusions from the qualitative material obtained in depth research is relatively mechanical. You can follow a straightforward process, such as the one described above, to develop concepts and identify patterns, then generalize them into a set of conclusions. The key challenge is to keep conclusions from being too general or "academic." Usually clients will not be happy with, or happy paying for, broad, sweeping, or merely ungrounded conclusions. However, at least that is better than the old standby of the artless analyst, which is ending your analysis with some variation of the phrase, "more research is needed."

Insights

Obtaining key insights takes your analysis to the level of applied, pragmatic learning and, from that, generating genuine business insights or the equivalent. It takes conclusions a step further, to providing a basis for making practical sense of and doing something with the learnings and other results you have obtained. The analyst must not only have some degree of mastery over the tools of research and analysis but also substantive knowledge of the general market arena and the client's business, their resources, issues, and challenges. Similarly, analysis of employee research, legal research, political, community or policy research all can and, in my opinion, should be taken to this next level of "so what?"

One way to do this is to work backwards, starting with your client's research problem or issue in mind and then go through your conclusions, one by one, piece by piece, and query each of these, "How, if at all, does this relate to my client's issue?" By working out and writing out "what it means" for your clients, how it relates to understanding and doing something about their challenges, you can provide useful insights. For example, the fact that, younger households have increasingly abandoned landlines for smartphones and other mobile devices in order to save money and maximize convenience is a conclusion. That this could explain a declining trend in a traditional telephone company's overall number of subscribers would be a business insight. As another example, changes in gender roles and relative incomes can lead to insights into family and childrearing dynamics.

Caveat: today, "insights" is coming to be used in a different sense than the above, to refer to big "wows," "eureka moments." Honestly, I have only ever had a few insights at this level in my entire social science and marketing research career. My key marketing/market research insight is that people tend to make the same choices again and again on the basis of inertia more than (brand) loyalty or rational judgment. This piggybacks off of Al Goldman's realization that physicians tend to exhibit "prescribing inertia." It also suggests a Newtonian principle that customers and others will tend to do the same thing over and over until or unless driven to change by some kind of counter-force.

So, to be clear, don't expect to draw that level of insight from any particular depth research project. You need to ensure that you and your clients are using the term "insight" in the same way and that they don't expect you to come up with a "eureka moment" in every study.

Actionable recommendations

Actionability is the hallmark of a master depth research analyst. Whether you are doing market research (understanding market structure and dynamics), marketing research (helping clients develop marketing strategy and tactics or understand and address marketing challenges), evaluations research (evaluating programs and initiatives), employee, legal, policy, community, political, or other applied research, the bottom line is crafting actionable recommendations. It is the true, value-added level of applied qualitative analytics. Learning the alchemy of translating findings into actionable recommendations goes beyond drawing conclusions or even providing "business insights" and their equivalent in other applied contexts. This brings us full circle to the issue of "so what?"

That is, you take your insights a step further, into recommending how your client might apply those insights in real world situations in order to create solutions or other applications of what has been learned or discovered in your depth research. You cannot do that for them, nor is that the researcher's or analyst's role; rather, action application is the next step beyond analysis, although it might well be your responsibility in a follow-on consulting engagement or, perhaps, as part of your overall role in an organization or agency. The analyst's domain extends to providing guidance — the more concrete and specific the better — on how the knowledge and insights gained from the analysis can be applied to solve relevant problems, overcome challenges, solve, or at least mitigate, hurdles, maximize results, or otherwise achieve the strategic objectives that prompted your clients to commission marketing research. This is the mountaintop level of value-added qualitative research.

Telling the story

It has become virtually commonplace to talk about "telling the story" with your analysis. I agree enthusiastically that the master analyst finds the story in the material, then organizes and marshals the material to tell that story. But I don't mean a story in the sense of a fiction writer or fabulist, more like that of a journalist.

I am not suggesting that you look for dramatic tension and resolution, identify archetypical characters, none of that. I am talking about finding and conveying the meaning of all the information you have gathered in depth research, with reference to your clients or end users of the learnings

— the "so what." And then breaking it down into sensible parts, call them chapters or sections or whatever, so that when you have worked through them in order, your conclusions, insights, and recommendations are not only fully supported but seem only natural, obvious, and inevitable. The idea is to array your facts and findings in a logical sequence that drives to that end. It doesn't matter whether you follow the discussion guide order (I almost invariably end up switching that around, at least a bit) or use some other ordering logic. You want your analysis to tease out and tell the story of your findings.

This book is not about writing the actual report; how to tell a non-fiction story that effectively communicates to and engages your specific audience is outside the scope of this book. Nevertheless, always remember that data and facts do not speak for themselves. You need to find and tell the story to your audience to accomplish the true ends of social scientific analysis.

Final thoughts on the analysis of depth research

There you have it, a distillation of over a quarter century of practice in designing, conducting, and analyzing depth research. By all means, you should dig further into the subject; there are many books and courses available. However, keep in mind that all the "book learning" in the world is no substitute for experiential learning and that there is no single "right way" to go about it. Every researcher brings a unique set of skills, sensibilities, perspectives, personal biography, knowledge, interests, and experiences to bear, and will find his or her own best way to do and analyze depth research. Enjoy your journey!

REFERENCES

Barber, T. X. (2013) *Pitfalls in Human Research: Ten Pivotal Points.* Burlington: Elsevier Science.

Blumer, H. (1986) *Symbolic Interactionism: Perspective and Method.* Berkeley, CA: University of California Press.

Bystedt, J., Lynn, S., and Potts, D. (2003, 2011) *Moderating to the Max: A Full-tilt Guide to Creative, Insightful Focus Groups and Depth Interviews.* Rochester, NY: Paramount Market Publishing, Inc.

Charmaz, K. (2014) *Constructing Grounded Theory, Second Edition.* Los Angeles: Sage.

Dale, J. and Abbott, S. (2014) *Qual-Online: The Essential Guide.* Rochester, NY: Paramount Market Publishing, Inc.

Featherstone, L. (2018) *Divining Desire: Focus Groups and the Culture of Consultation.* New York: OR Books.

Garfinkle, H. (1967). *Studies in Ethnomethodology.* Englewood Cliffs, NJ: Prentice-Hall.

Glaser, B.G. and Strauss, A.L. (1967) *The Discovery of Grounded Theory: Strategies for Qualitative Research.* New York: Aldine Publishing.

Goffman, E. (1959) *The Presentation of Self In Everyday Life.* New York: Anchor Books.

Goffman, E. (1952) "On Cooling the Mark Out." *Psychiatry: Journal of Interpersonal Relations* vol. 15, 451–463.

Goldman, A.E. (1962) "The Group Depth Interview." *The Journal of Marketing,* vol. 26, no. 3: 61–68.

Goldman, A.E. and McDonald, S.S. (1987) *The Group Depth Interview: Principles and Practice.* Englewood Cliffs, NJ: Prentice-Hall.

Harris, David F. (2014) *The Complete Guide to Writing Questionnaires: How to Get Better Information for Better Decisions.* Durham, NC: I&M Press.

Kaufman, M.T. (2003) "Robert K. Merton, Versatile Sociologist and Father of the Focus Group, Dies at 92." *The New York Times.* merton-versatile-sociologist-and-father-of-the-focus-group-dies-at-92.html. Retrieved 10 December 2009.

Kotler, P. and Keller, K.L. (2009) *Marketing Management.* 13th ed., Upper Saddle River, NJ: Pearson.

Krippendorff, K. (2004) *Content Analysis: An Introduction to Its Methodology.* 2nd ed., Thousand Oaks, CA: Sage Publishing.

Lofland, J., Snow, D.A., Anderson, L., and Lofland, L. (2005) *Analyzing Social Settings: A Guide to Qualitative Observation and Analysis.* 4th ed. Mason, OH: South-Western Cengage Learning.

Mason, M. (2010) *Sample Size and Saturation in PhD Studies Using Qualitative Interviews.* Forum Qualitative Sozialforschung / Forum: Qualitative Social Research, [S.l.], vol. 11, no. 3, August 2010. ISSN 1438-5627. Available at: http://www.qualitative-research.net/index.php/fqs/article/view/1428/3027. Retrieved: 31 August 2018.

Merton, R.K., Lowenthal, M.F., and Kendall, P.L. (1990) *The Focused Interview: A Manual of Problems and Procedures.* 2nd ed. New York: The Free Press.

Mira, A. (2010) *Defining Pragmatics.* Cambridge: Cambridge University Press.

Osborn, A.F. (1963) *Applied Imagination: Principles and Procedures of Creative Problem Solving.* Third Revised ed. New York: Charles Scribner's Sons.

Pepper, S.C. (1970) *World Hypotheses: A Study in Evidence.* Berkeley, CA: University of California Press.

Ramaswamyh, V. and Gouillart, F. (2010) *The Power of Co-Creation: Build It with Them to Boost Growth, Productivity and Profits.* New York: Free Press.

Schatzman,L. and Strauss, A. (1973) *Field Research: Strategies for a Natural Sociology.* Englewood Cliffs, N.J.: Prentice-Hall.

Sherman, B.S. and Straus, R.A. (2002) "Noticing, Questioning, Explaining: Research Methods." Chapter 3 in *Using Sociology: An Introduction From the Applied and Clinical Perspectives.* 3rd ed. pp. 45-85. Lanham, MD: Rowman and Littlefield.

Straus, R.A. (Editor) (2002) U*sing Sociology: An Introduction From the Applied and Clinical Perspectives.* 3rd ed. Lantham, MD: Rowman and Littlefield.

Straus, R.A. (2000) *Creative Self-Hypnosis.* Bloomington, IN: iUniverse.

Straus, R.A. (2000) Strategic Self-Hypnosis. Revised Edition, Bloomington, IN: iUniverse.

Tema-Lyn, L. (2011) *Stir It Up! Recipes for Robust Insights & Red Hot Ideas.* Rochester, NY: Paramount Market Publishing, Inc.

About the Author

Roger A. Straus, Ph.D. has over twenty-five years of experience as a marketing researcher and sociological practitioner. A Certified Clinical Sociologist, he currently divides his time between his role as a Vice President with the Blackstone Group, Inc. and his independent consulting practice. He previously served as a research executive with such leading custom research houses as GfK, TVG, Opinion Research Corporation, and National Analysts Division of Booz Allen Hamilton.

In addition to countless focus groups, depth interviews and other qualitative studies, Dr. Straus has been responsible for a large number of quantitative surveys, typically involving advanced analytics. He has provided domestic and global research to a wide range of clients from Fortune 100 companies across industry verticals to universities, professional associations and start-ups. Dr. Straus has also served as head of Market Insight for ZymoGenetics, now a Division of Bristol-Myers Squibb.

Growing up in Great Neck, New York, he attended Antioch College in Ohio and the New School for Social Research in New York City, then moved to the West Coast. After receiving his Ph.D. in Sociology from the University of California, Davis, with a specialization in qualitative methodology, Dr. Straus decided to apply social science to solving real-world problems. He co-founded what is now the Association for Applied and Clinical Sociology, and remains an internationally recognized leader in the emerging field of sociological practice. He has published many articles on marketing research and social science, two textbooks on sociological practice, and a number of books for clinicians and the general public, one of which has been a best-seller. He has taught at the University of California, Alfred University, the MBA program at Maryhurst University, and elsewhere.

After many years in the Philadelphia area, he moved to Portland, Oregon, in 2006. Just to keep things interesting, he assists his wife with her independent music labels focusing on good-time Americana music. Currently mammal-free, they live with a number of koi, tropical fish, and an extremely personable box turtle.